* persuasive presentations

how to get the response you need

CREATIVE BUSINESS SOLUTIONS

*persuasive presentations

how to get the response you need nick souter

artwork by guy billout

ILEX

First published in the United Kingdom in 2007 by

I L E X

The Old Candlemakers
West Street
Lewes
East Sussex BN7 2NZ
www.ilex-press.com

Publisher: Alastair Campbell
Creative Director: Peter Bridgewater
Associate Publisher: Robin Pearson
Editorial Director: Tom Mugridge
Editor: Ben Renow-Clarke
Art Director: Julie Weir
Designer: Jonathan Raimes
Design Assistant: Kate Haynes

Artwork © Guy Billout

British Library Cataloguing-in-Publication Data
A catalogue record for this book is available from
the British Library

ISBN 10: 1-905814-11-9
ISBN 13: 978-1-905814-11-4

For more information on this title, go to:
www.web-linked.com/bpreuk

Printed and bound in China

contents

CD-ROM Contents

There are four interactive software tools on the attached CD-ROM.

They are:

1. **The Planning Model**. This tool will ensure you consider every vital element of your presentation.
2. **The 5 Whys**. This process will ensure you talk about benefits and not merely features.
3. **The Information Map**. This software will organize your thoughts into themes that support your purpose.
4. **The Organizational Diamond**. This system imposes a structure that will make your presentation more persuasive.

1. How to use this book

Presentations are the daily rituals of business life. In these forums, both large and small, we give and receive information, sell our ideas, and lay the groundwork for important decisions. Despite the constant hum of digital communication, we spend more and more of our lives in these face-to-face interactions.

Studies in America suggest that when you take a first step on the corporate ladder, you spend around 25% of your working day in a meeting room. Climb to middle management and that figure doubles. And if you reach the dizzying heights of the executive rungs, you'll be giving or listening to presentations for 75% of your time.

Presentations are how we do business. And if you are going to climb that ladder, you must deliver presentations that are engaging, lucid, and persuasive.

Frequently, your ability and value to the company will be judged not so much on what you do, but on how well you can explain what you do.
And what you want others to do.

Unfortunately, not many of us like standing up and speaking in public. If research is to be believed, it's our No. 1 fear and outranks even death and poverty. (Comedian Jerry Seinfeld quips that an American asked to deliver the eulogy at a funeral would prefer to be in the coffin!)

This nervousness has led many people to believe that public speaking is a gift. You either have it or you don't. If that is your concern then rest assured: persuasion is a competency and one you can learn. It's a process. After reading this book you will be able to plan, prepare, and deliver a persuasive presentation. If you practice, you will become skillful in leading an audience to a point where they understand and agree with your beliefs and recommendations.

The secret lies in planning and preparation.

Rarely, if ever, does a presentation exceed the quality of the planning process that precedes it.

When you decide what to put into a presentation, you are effectively deciding what the audience will take out of it. And therein lies the power of persuasion, because you can exert total control over that material.

This book is based on the structure it intends to teach. It's a concept that dates back to the 3rd century BC when Aristotle was establishing the "Five Principles of Rhetoric" at the Lyceum in Ancient Greece. Learning from Socrates and Plato before him, Aristotle taught his students that **structure is the scaffolding that enables us to build a persuasive argument.**

It is structure that supports our ideas and beliefs and enables us to lead an audience to the conclusion we want them to reach. Over more than 2,000 years, Aristotle's principles have stood the test of time. They remain as relevant and effective today as when he first conceived them.

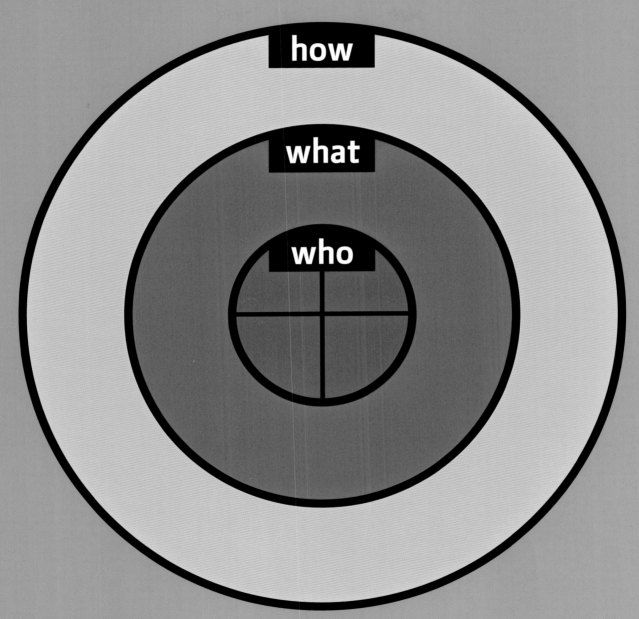

The Planning Model

The illustration on the previous page shows the framework of the Planning Model we intend to use. From this we will develop a process that takes you from initial preparation through detailed planning and then to the delivery of a persuasive presentation.

As you can see, there are three areas we are going to study:

the "Who," the "What," and the "How."

Unless you are talking to yourself (and that's not uncommon in business presentations), there are never less than two parties involved in any communication. In the first section, the Who, we will learn how to analyze both the speaker and the listener to ensure that the message being sent is the one being received. It's not always the case that what is being said is what is being heard.
We'll use a Communication Model called "Seeing Eye to Eye" that looks at how our messages are often distorted by the thoughts and prejudices of the audience. We'll then work with the Herrmann Brain Dominance Instrument to see how we can protect the integrity of our message by adapting our style, language, and content to suit the communication preferences of our listeners.

Once we understand how to tune into our audience's wavelength and communicate clearly, we'll move onto the What. This section looks at what it is we want to say and what we hope to achieve by saying it.
Most presentations fail because they don't have a clearly defined purpose. We'll look at how you can define and refine the purpose of your presentation so that it becomes the criterion by which you judge its content.
Once your purpose is established we can look at different methods of gathering and selecting information. What do you use and what do you lose? This is where Aristotle's schema can impose a structure that connects the relevant information to your purpose in such a way that it becomes persuasive.

Lastly, we'll look at the How. How do we control verbal and non-verbal communication? How do we talk? How do we stand, how do we move? How do we use visual aids to support our message? How do we control our nerves?

The How looks at all the practicalities of delivering the presentation. It takes an argument that has been carefully structured and assembled on paper and turns it into a living, emotionally charged, interactive experience that will capture the imagination of everyone in the room.

The *Who* and the *What* give you a script.
The *How* turns it into a performance.

The Planning Model is depicted as concentric circles because we want to stress that the trinity of Who, What, and How are not so much connected as inseparable.

That doesn't mean you can't dip in and out of this book and use it as a collection of useful tips and reminders, but when planning a presentation, you need to work through every stage of the process. This version of Aristotle's structure will support your argument and will support you while you deliver it. But if part of it is missing, then your presentation will be weakened.

You may be tempted to save time by skipping some of the steps. But there's no need. We've found that

most people save up to 50% of their preparation time by working through the Planning Model.

Not only does it force you to be more efficient in delivering your ideas, it helps you be more efficient in collecting, sifting, and organizing them.

So let's start at the beginning of the process and work our way right through to the end.

We'll begin by asking two questions:

"Who am I?"

"Who is listening?"

2. The Who:

Who's talking?
Who's listening?

Communication

Have you ever had the disturbing feeling that someone is listening to you but not actually hearing what you are saying? They speak your language, they have an interest in the subject you are discussing, and yet your words are failing to "reach" them.

In such a situation, persuasion cannot take place because communication is not taking place.

So what exactly do we mean by communication?

The *Collins English Dictionary* defines it as:

"The imparting of thoughts, feelings, or ideas."

In the context of the workplace it's perhaps better described as:

"The exchange of information—the getting or giving of facts; gaining agreement—getting or giving approval; developing goodwill—building or exchanging trust."

Or in Aristotle's words:

"Who says what to whom and with what effect."

The common theme in these definitions is that communication is a two-way process. It involves an exchange. It is more than just words because it involves actions and feelings and requires the conveyance of meaning and understanding.

So what is happening when someone is listening to you but not actually hearing what you are saying? It is possible that they just don't understand you. But what if they understand your words perfectly and yet your message is still not getting through?

The illustration opposite looks like the blueprint for a Big Mac but is actually what we call the

"Seeing Eye to Eye" Communication Model.

Communicator A

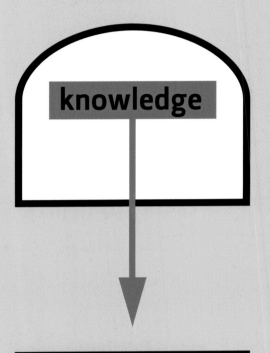

knowledge

knowledge

Communicator B

The "Seeing Eye to Eye" Communication Model

In any conversation there are at least two communicators. We've called them A and B. As you'll see in this diagram, each has his own store of knowledge—facts, ideas, information, beliefs, and so on.

The object of the exercise is for communicator A to get his message into the mind of communicator B. Later in the process we'll see a reversal and communicator B will send back his response.

For effective communication to take place, communicator B will have to receive the message in the exact form that communicator A intended. Otherwise there will be a misunderstanding.

However, there are obstacles in the path of this process. If you look at the first illustration on the following page you'll see that both communicators, A and B, have their own individual experiences of life—different upbringings, different philosophies, different ideas. These experiences form the lenses through which they see the world and through which they see and receive knowledge and information.

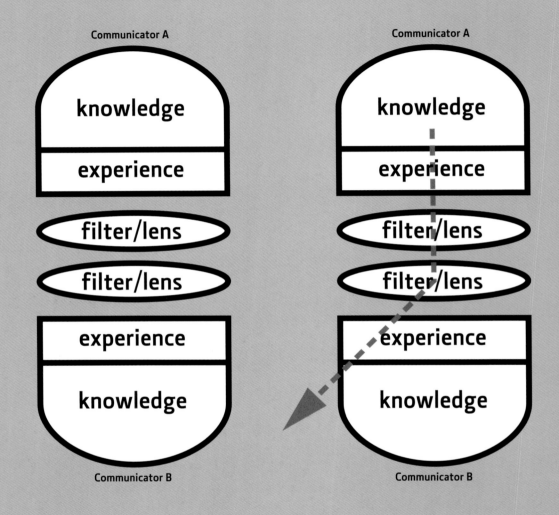

Communicator A

knowledge

experience

filter/lens

filter/lens

experience

knowledge

Communicator B

Communicator A

knowledge

experience

filter/lens

filter/lens

experience

knowledge

Communicator B

Seeing through lenses

Communication distortion

The interesting thing about lenses is that we forget that we are wearing them. We don't notice the lens, we just look though it. A simple analogy would be wearing glasses. We put them on and forget them. We then see the world looks as we expect it to look. Clear.

Our unique experience of life, our ideas and experiences filter and distort what we see and hear. To quote Anaïs Nin:

"We see the world not as it is, but as we are."

Two people looking at the same bottle of water will see the same bottle. But if one of them is dying of thirst and the other has just been rescued from drowning, they'll "see" the bottle in very different ways.

Prejudice is a great example of how our lenses distort reality.

Imagine I want to buy a pair of shoes. But, from my life experience, I have learned to distrust salespeople—I think they care more about their commission than they do about me. (This belief may not be related to shoes at all. Perhaps a car salesman persuaded me to buy a car that didn't suit my needs and now I don't trust salesmen.)

I go to the shoe store and the salesman recommends a pair of shoes that are more expensive than those I intended to buy. He explains that these shoes are made from the finest leather, are hand-tooled, are guaranteed for five years, are waterproof, oil-proof, scuff-proof, and extremely comfortable due to a revolutionary and proprietary process that allows the sole to bend without making it weak. When I try them on, he says they look great and really suit me.

What happens to his communication is described in the second illustration on the opposite page. He is communicator A and I am the receiver, communicator B.

What he says leaves his mouth and starts the difficult journey to my mind. Everything he says is consistent with his own experience and beliefs and so it passes through his own filters and lenses without distortion. (He's probably not aware of this happening. He's forgotten his own lenses.)

But then his message hits my lens, my filter. This is the filter that says, "Don't trust salesmen. They just want your money."

He says, "This is the best shoe for you." The words go through my filter and I hear, "This is the most expensive shoe and I get the most commission on it."

He says, "This shoe comes with a five-year guarantee." I hear, "This is the most expensive shoe and I get the most commission on it."

He says, "This shoe is hand-made, using only the finest leather." I hear, "This is the most expensive shoe and I get the most commission on it."

And so on.

I listen to his words, I may even nod my head in agreement, but I'm hearing something completely different.

Of course the same miscommunication can take place when I respond. He is used to people stalling for time and not buying. Perhaps I'm dressed in such a way as to suggest I might not be able to afford the shoes he's selling.

I say, "I need to think about it." That perfectly reasonable message hits his filter or lens and is transformed. He hears, "He doesn't want to spend the money."

I say, "I'm going to try on a different pair." He hears, "He doesn't want to spend the money."

And so on.

For successful communication to take place, and particularly if we want that communication to be persuasive and create change in the mind of the listener, we need to recognize one another's reality lenses and filters so that we can tailor our presentation to avoid refraction and distortion.

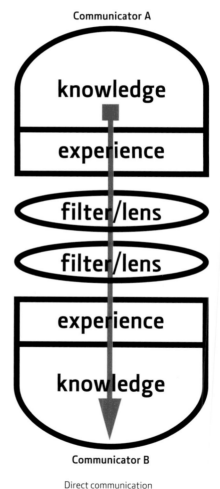

Direct communication

When we can do that, we'll achieve the communication described in the illustration opposite. What we say travels directly, and without distortion, to the mind of our listener where it can be assessed. In other words they believe us and are "open to persuasion."

In my encounter with the shoe salesman, he could have benefited from knowing my prejudice and reality lenses. Then he could have gained my trust by showing me a cheaper pair of shoes first and then seeing if he could up-sell me to a more expensive pair after a good rapport and clear line of communication had been established.

And that is exactly what a good salesman does whether he is in a showroom or a boardroom.

To borrow an adage from the world of advertising, "A good salesman doesn't 'sell,' he makes you want to buy." And he does that by knowing how to get past your filters and prejudices.

This becomes more complicated when talking to a room full of people, as there will be many different lenses bending your message out of shape. Clearly, we need a system for understanding the audience so that we can adopt the right attitudes and language.

The ancient Greeks were well aware of this issue. In Aristotle's day, they established the personality of the audience by plotting them on two intersecting continuums. One led from Sanguine to Melancholic, which today we would describe as Optimistic to Pessimistic. The other led from Choleric to Phlegmatic, which we would probably characterize as Angry to Calm.

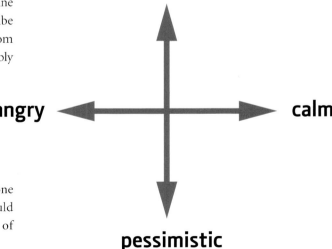

By deciding where the audience lay between one axis and the other, students of Aristotle could determine the appropriate style and tenor of their presentation.

This science of personality profiling has developed a great deal in recent years. In 1923, the psychologist Carl Jung decided humanity could be divided into two categories— Introverts and Extroverts. The former are inward-looking whereas the latter focus on the world outside of themselves.

His work was further developed by the team of Myers and Briggs who introduced yet another axis—Judges and Perceivers. Judges seek control through order and closure while Perceivers are more open-minded and tend to take life as it comes.

The combination of these two perspectives led to MBTI—the Myers Briggs Type Indicator. This system has become very popular with the Human Resources departments of large corporations. Chances are, if you've applied for a job with a multinational company, you will have been subjected to this sort of profiling.

Much as we all like to think of ourselves as individuals, intrinsically different and interesting, we do belong to clearly defined groups or "types." Most people who have been through MBTI are astonished by how accurate it is in defining their likes and dislikes and predicting how they will react and behave in certain situations. This makes it an extremely useful tool when trying to decide if someone is suitable for a certain type of work and whether they will fit in well with the team.

It is by no means the only personality-profiling tool. In recent years we've come across DISC, Personalysis, and Emergenetics to name just three of the systems that offer profound insights into the behavior and attitude of different personalities.

For our purpose, which is to understand our audience, we need something that is simple and intuitive. For that reason, we use HBDI— the Herrmann Brain Dominance Indicator.

But it's not just the audience we need to understand. As we said earlier, communication is a two-way process. Both parties have preferences in the way they like to give and receive information.

As well as understanding our audience, we need to understand ourselves. HBDI can help.

It's also important to recognize that nobody is entirely one color. We have varying degrees of preference in all of the quadrants. But it's quite usual for one to dominate to the extent that it describes us.

The Green Quadrant

The lower left, green quadrant is a combination of the left brain's logic and the mammalian brain's emotions and feelings. People whose thinking preferences are located in this quadrant will tend to be "Organizers."

How do we recognize them?

They are cautious.

True Greens will never give you a knee-jerk response.

They want to consider every aspect of the situation very carefully before committing themselves to a point of view or course of action.

They love process and systems. In a presentation they want to start with an agenda and follow that with a step-by-step delivery of the information.

They are highly risk averse. The Green quadrant is all about safekeeping. To that end, they want alignment with established procedures and a clearly structured action plan that states who is accountable for every stage of the process. To avoid unpleasant surprises, they will study all of the background information and will want an assurance that what you are proposing has been done before.

"Organizers" will struggle with ambiguity, uncertain directions, and unclear expectations. You'll lose them immediately if you suggest they take a chance on something. They'd rather drink poison than "suck it and see."

The good thing about working with Greens is that they are very buttoned-down. They know their stuff and are all over the details. They turn up on time and rarely over-run.

The downside is that they can be anal-retentive and only see the "small picture." They see the trees not the forest and this can make it hard to steer them onto the path you'd like to take.

The tell-tale sign in their office is tidiness. Expect an empty desk with just the necessary papers at hand.

Once again, before we move on, make a list of five Green quadrant "Organizers" you have known.

Five Greens

1................................
2................................
3................................
4................................
5................................

The Red Quadrant

The lower right, red quadrant is an overlap of the right brain's imaginative powers with the mammalian brain's emotional system. People whose thinking preferences are located in this quadrant will tend to be "Sensors."

How do we recognize them?

The Reds, as the color suggests, are a passionate group, and will react spontaneously to your plans and proposals.

They are "People" people. They like group discussion and personal connections. They like to share their ideas and express their feelings. It's important to them that a meeting or a presentation is a user-friendly learning experience. They value harmony, and expect empathy and consideration of their needs.

In return, they are extremely intuitive and will be equally considerate of your feelings. They'll always meet your eye and treat you with respect.

"Sensors" will struggle with too much data and analysis. As they value personal interaction, they don't want a lecture that inhibits their participation. They want a dialog and continuous feedback.

The good thing about working with Reds is that they are sensitive to everyone involved. Their "touchy-feely" approach promotes good teamwork and a positive environment.

The downside is that they are not always in control of their emotions. When the facts get in the way of feelings, enthusiasm can turn to frustration and anger.

You'll know you are in the office of a Red quadrant thinker by the number of photos, mementos, and keepsakes that adorn the desk and walls. You'll get a biscuit as well as the coffee and there'll be plenty of time allowed for getting to know one another.

Scour your memory and find five Red quadrant "Sensors" you know. You may notice that they tend to be women whereas the Blues tend to be men.

Five Reds

1.................................

2.................................

3.................................

4.................................

5.................................

The Yellow Quadrant

The upper right, yellow quadrant is the synthesis of the right brain's imagination and the intellect of the front brain's neocortex. People whose thinking preferences are located in this quadrant will tend to be "Explorers."

How do we recognize them?

Easily.

Yellow quadrant thinkers love to experiment and will always react thoughtfully to a proposal as they search for new and interesting opportunities within it.

They love fun and spontaneity, a quick pace and variety. Attention span is not their strong point and so they need constant stimulation.

Rather than a step-by-step presentation, they enjoy an overview and conceptual framework so that they can then explore the material and not be limited by a structure you impose.

They are very visual. They need imagery and metaphors, and prefer to learn experientially. Any recommendation you make needs to inspire and excite their imagination. Literally and metaphorically, Yellows hate boxes and they don't try to check them.

The good thing about working with Yellows is that they see the "big picture." They are quick to synthesize ideas and great at getting things started. They are fearless and always prepared to experiment and take risks. They have boundless enthusiasm for any proposal that lets them try something new. And they have wonderful imaginations.

But the downside is that they are disorganized. You'll see that from the "mad professor" style of their office space. And if you think it's messy on their desk, you'll find the same chaos in their heads.

Yellow quadrant thinkers have poor time management skills and are bad at meeting deadlines. They hate administrative tasks and, whenever possible, skimp on details. They have poor follow-through and frequently leave tasks unfinished. They get bored easily and lose interest and motivation.

List five Yellow quadrant "Explorers" you know.

Five Yellows

1................................
2................................
3................................
4................................
5................................

While searching your mind for good examples, you have probably noticed that some of your friends and colleagues display strong characteristics from more than one quadrant. This is perfectly normal. Many people are "double dominant" which means that, when they are tested by the Herrmann questionnaire, they display preferences in two quadrants. It's possible to be triple dominant or even "whole-brained," which suggests equal ease in all four thinking quadrants.

Before we look at how these quadrants get along with one another, we need to see where you stand in relation to them.

What are you? Blue, Green, Red, or Yellow?

For the moment, let's take a snapshot of how you operate and get a rough feel of where you are on the Herrmann model.

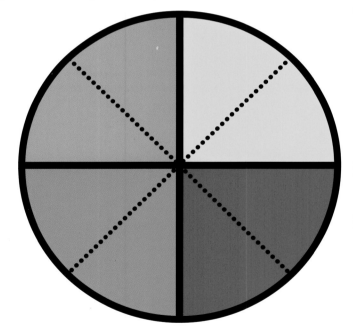

This illustration shows an empty set of quadrants with a calibration line bisecting each. Start with the Blue box and, using the dots on the calibration line, give yourself a mark 1–10 of how much you feel you conform to the thinking preferences and style of the Blues.

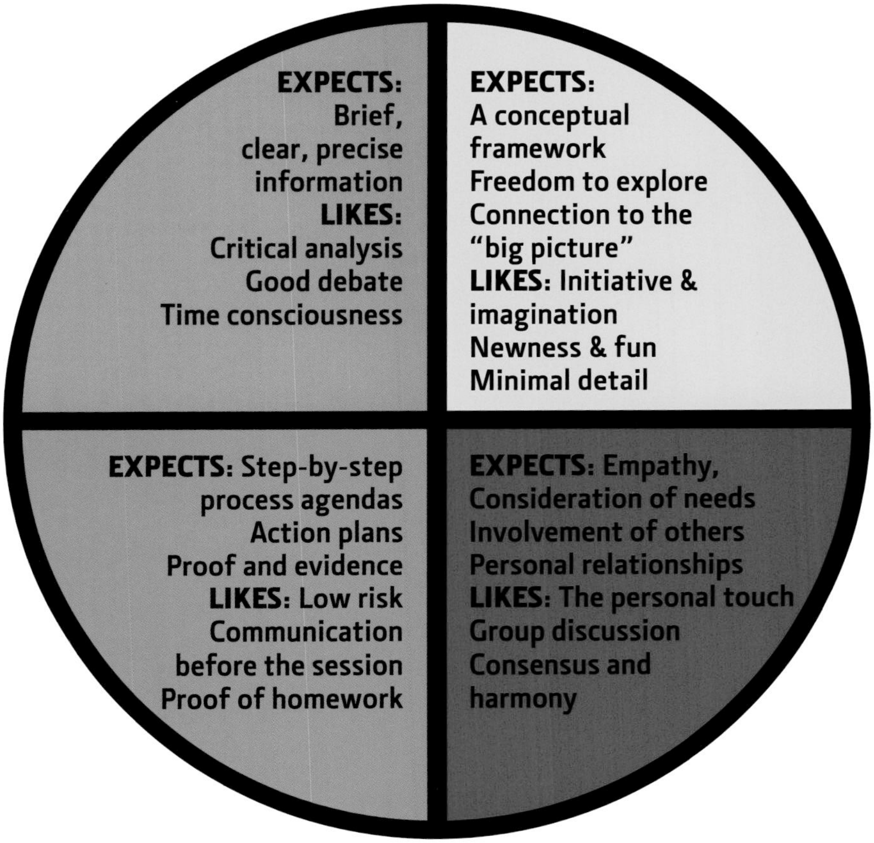

EXPECTS:
Brief,
clear, precise
information
LIKES:
Critical analysis
Good debate
Time consciousness

EXPECTS:
A conceptual
framework
Freedom to explore
Connection to the
"big picture"
LIKES: Initiative &
imagination
Newness & fun
Minimal detail

EXPECTS: Step-by-step
process agendas
Action plans
Proof and evidence
LIKES: Low risk
Communication
before the session
Proof of homework

EXPECTS: Empathy,
Consideration of needs
Involvement of others
Personal relationships
LIKES: The personal touch
Group discussion
Consensus and
harmony

The illustration above will remind you of the key characteristics of each quadrant. Then work your way counterclockwise around the model and mark yourself in each quadrant.

Then join up the dots. You should end up with a shape that looks similar to the images on the next page.

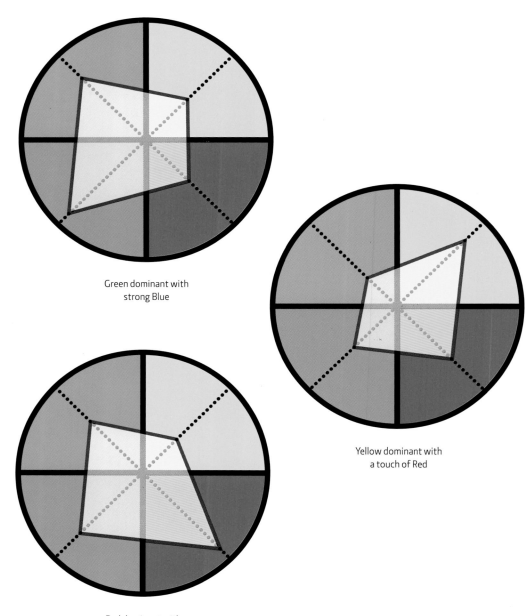

Green dominant with
strong Blue

Yellow dominant with
a touch of Red

Red dominant with
a touch of Green and Blue

This crude profile will help us understand how to modify your natural presenting style so that you can get onto your audience's wavelength. We need to align your style with theirs so that we can reduce the sort of distortion we saw in the "Seeing Eye to Eye" model.

The necessity for this becomes very clear when you look at how the different quadrants interact with one another. For example, Blue and Red are diametrically opposed. As are Yellow and Green.

Imagine a chance conversation between Blue and Red where Blue instigates the exchange.

Blue: "Hi. How are you?"

Red: "I'm fine."

Blue: "Great, we need to meet and discuss…."

Blue hears the words and reacts and continues accordingly.

But what if Red were to lead the conversation?

Red: "Hi. How are you?"

Blue: "I'm fine."

Red: "Really. You seem a bit under the weather. Are you sure…?"

Red hears the words but feels them as well.

Blue may seem cold to Red. Red may seem gushy and oversensitive to Blue. Either way, lenses are now refracting the communication between them. They see each other as different even though they have both answered the same question with the same words.

We can see a similar dissonance between Yellow and Green.

When Yellow says, "This is a great idea. No one has done this before!" Green reacts with horror and thinks, "This is going to be a terrible risk."
And that's before he's even heard the idea.

And if Green says, "Let's go through this one step at a time," Yellow starts to yawn and think about something else.

But while the diametric opposites are clearly different, the adjacent quadrants always have some shared characteristics and sympathy for one another.

Red and Yellow have the underlying connection of being part of the right brain and are both intuitive.

Green and Blue share a left-brain concern with facts. But while one values analysis, the other favors process.

Blue: "Give me a one-pager, a top line, and the necessary information and I'll tell you what I think."

Green: "Give me all the information and I'll take it home and go through it. I'll get back to you tomorrow and tell you what I decide and which is the best option. By the way, there's a typo in the first paragraph."

Blue and Red share an intellect.
One uses it for analysis, the other for conceptualization.
Green and Red share an emotional bias.
But one is concerned with systems while the other is worrying about humanity.

With a little practice, you'll find it becomes quick and easy to guess where someone is situated on the model. Look at the diagram on page 38 to see some of the values that each quadrant is concerned with.

This short exercise will help.

Decide on your dominant quadrant and then choose a friend or colleague from the diametrically opposed one. Now list five areas of potential conflict you might perceive between yourself and them.

For example, I was continually at loggerheads with my business partner in advertising. He was Green and Blue and I am strongly Red and Yellow.

We conflicted over:

1. **Timekeeping**
2. **Attention to detail**
3. **Follow-through**
4. **Risk assessment**
5. **Staff selection**

He was all about "How to" and I was all about "What if?" My job put me in charge of developing new ideas for our company's clients. I quickly learned that if we were to communicate effectively so that I could get my agenda up and running, then I would have to structure my presentations to allow for his thinking preferences.

That meant selling imaginative and untested ideas by creating a presentation framework that explored timelines, accountability, cost, a plan B, and an explanation of why I had chosen a particular team to complete the assignment. Basically, I had to travel down my own corpus callosum and recruit the under-used services of my Green and Blue competencies.

Only then could he really hear what I wanted to say and needed him to understand.

By removing a clash of styles, I removed much of the distortion that could have blurred our communication.

The Herrmann model gives us a simple process to help us see eye to eye.

1. Understand your audience's communication style.
2. Understand your own communication style.
3. Align the two so that you reduce the refraction of one another's lenses.

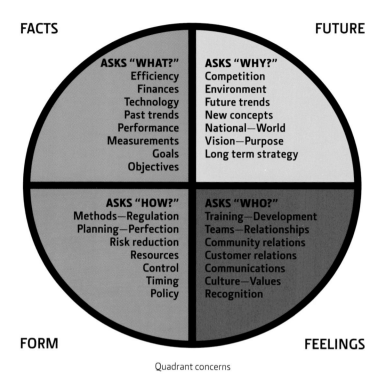

FACTS   FUTURE

ASKS "WHAT?"
Efficiency
Finances
Technology
Past trends
Performance
Measurements
Goals
Objectives

ASKS "WHY?"
Competition
Environment
Future trends
New concepts
National—World
Vision—Purpose
Long term strategy

ASKS "HOW?"
Methods—Regulation
Planning—Perfection
Risk reduction
Resources
Control
Timing
Policy

ASKS "WHO?"
Training—Development
Teams—Relationships
Community relations
Customer relations
Communications
Culture—Values
Recognition

FORM   FEELINGS

Quadrant concerns

Just to complicate things, the audience's style is a composite of many different personal styles and your presentation has to reflect an understanding of that.

Imagine you are presenting to a boardroom of predominantly Blue quadrant accountants but one of the key decision-makers just happens to have a strong streak of Red in his thinking. Most of them are worrying about the numbers, but he's worrying about the people.

Majority rule doesn't apply in this situation. You will have to structure your presentation in a way that appeals to them all.

This is not as tricky as it sounds. Awareness is the key. Once you have identified the needs of your audience, you'll find that the organizational structure we use in the next section, The How, is sufficiently flexible to help you address a diverse range of thinking styles.

But in all of this, there is one constant. YOU.

Let's look more closely at how you behave when addressing a group of people you want to influence or persuade.

Understanding Your "Act"

We all have an act. We all have a particular way of presenting ourselves to others.

It usually changes from one situation to the next. We may have an act for our friends and family but a slightly different one for our coworkers and clients. (How often have you found yourself feeling differently about a colleague once you have spent time with him or her outside of your working environment or with their family and friends?) This may sound as if we are false and affected. But that is not actually the case. We are social animals and we have an innate ability to behave in ways that gain us entry and secure our position within different groups. If we can't do this, we are usually regarded as inflexible and socially inept.

Differing acts do not require differing selves. The integrity of the self is not in question here. When we change our act we do not change our values, attitudes, or beliefs. (That would be false.) We merely change the way we present them. In fact, in any given situation, your act is not a chameleon-like attempt to hide. It's the opposite. It's the embodiment of a character that gives you the comfort and security to reveal yourself, your thoughts, and your ideas.

Understanding your act is important for two reasons. First, once you recognize it, you'll be able to use and control it.

Secondly, your act can protect you from the bouts of nerves so many of us fear when speaking in public. (We'll look at how controlling your act can achieve this in the section on anxiety management in Chapter 4.)

What matters now is to develop an understanding of how your act affects others.

So how do you define it?

It's easier to get someone to define it for you. Some years ago I attended a seminar based on the material in this book. Over two days we practiced the skills of making persuasive presentations. By the end of day one, my act was revealed.

I was tagged "The Irreverent Professor."

That doesn't sound like the most charismatic persona for persuasive speaking. But it works for me if I embrace it as my natural style.

Like most people, I have a nervousness about getting up and standing in the spotlight. One way I have compensated for this over the years is to ensure that I have really studied my material. In preparation for a presentation I absorb myself in the facts. In fact, I wrap them around me like armor. Despite being pretty much a Yellow and Red quadrant person, I fall back on my Blue quadrant competencies when I'm under pressure. I suspect it's this tendency that gives me a slightly professorial air.

But on the other hand, I don't take myself too seriously. I like to poke fun and deflate the pressure of a presentation by taking sideswipes at anything I think is pretentious or absurd—hence the "irreverent" part.

The value of knowing this is that I can turn the volume up and down on this behavior without having to change myself to the point where I cease to be me.

It's essential when we make a presentation that we stick with our act and remain "in character." Otherwise we will most definitely seem false and affected. But at the same time it's important to be able to "direct" our act so that it works for the audience. Being a professor and being irreverent are both styles that exist on a sliding scale. Now that I understand that these are my natural tendencies, I can adjust them accordingly and make sure that I stay on the right wavelength for the people who are listening.

What you have to say will be distorted and refracted if the audience feels your "act" is wrong for the occasion.

If you seem inappropriate, everything you say will seem inappropriate. And so, once again, we need to align our behavior with the audience's needs and expectations. That way our messages will get through.

The best way to determine your act is to ask your partners. When rehearsing for a presentation, get everyone in the room to watch you and tell you how you come across. Find out what sort of impression you make.

Alternatively, get someone to video you and then watch it. This may be a cringe-making prospect, but force yourself. It's never as bad as you expect. (Most people are relieved to discover that their nerves and crises of confidence are invisible to an observer.)

You are not looking for criticism of your presentation style and abilities. Being told you seem "nervous" or "confused" does not reveal your act. Those are just comments on your performance. We need to go deeper. You need to discover the essential character you portray when you are up on the stage. (We'll worry about performance later.)

It might help to think in terms of Adjectives, Roles, and Personalities.

For example:

Adjective-based:

A Sincere Act, An Honest Act, A Macho Act, A Caring Act, An Enthusiastic Act, and so on.

Role-based:

A Teacher's Act, a Coach's Act, A Professor's Act, A Little Girl's Act, A Newscaster's Act, and so on.

Personality-based:

An Anthony Robbins Act, A John Cleese Act, An Oprah Act, and so on.

People are complex and often it helps to combine adjectives and roles, as in my own case.

The Acts

1. The Story Teller
2. The Slick Professional
3. The Irreverent Professor
4. The Ditzy Blonde
5. The Good Cop
6. The King of Confidence
7. The Guru
8. The Bedside Manner
9. The Politician
10. The Fanatic
11. The Absent Minded Intellectual
12. The Cool, Calm, and Collected
13. The Enthusiast
14. The Caring Parent
15. The School Teacher
16. The Sincere Friend
17. The Rock Star
18. The Stand-up Comedian
19. The Foreign Correspondent
20. The Weird and Wonderful

The panel shown at left gives some examples of the acts we have seen while delivering our Persuasive Presentations course. Use them for inspiration when trying to understand your own.

Once you've defined it, you can start to work with it. Like an actor, learn how to project it. Learn how to vary the intensity of the qualities that make this act work for you.

Understanding Culture and Context

So far we have explored the forces that are acting on you and your audience from within.

We've looked at how communication can be distorted by the lenses that are worn by both speaker and listener. Using HBDI, we've understood how this refraction can be reduced by aligning our thinking preferences with those of the audience. In so doing, we can learn to speak in the way they want to listen.

We're now going to examine the external forces that affect the way our messages are received and interpreted. These fall into two groups: culture and context.

Culture

All intentional communities, be they churches or corporations, develop cultures that define and sustain them.

The *American Heritage Dictionary* defines culture as:

"The predominating attitudes and behavior that characterize the functioning of a group or organization."

This suggests that we can see and understand the culture of a company simply by observing it. However,

every company has a "Hidden" as well as a "Formal" culture.

If we are going to make a presentation that is persuasive, we need to understand both.

The Formal culture is the one you read about in the annual report. It states the company's values and ambitions, attitudes, and behaviors. For example, we might describe the Formal culture of Nike as "Fearless innovators at the cutting edge of sports fashion."

From this we might deduce that the team at Nike would welcome any presentation that advocates an innovative course of action. And we might be right.

Or perhaps we see The Body Shop as company that "Protects the natural world as well as your natural beauty."

Those cultural values would suggest that any proposal that is environmentally sensitive would be well received. And, again, that may well be so. I haven't worked with either company but I have a fairly strong sense of what they are about.

The important thing to note is that our understanding of a Formal culture comes directly from the company. It is what they want us to know about them. It's carefully aligned with the brand values expressed by their marketing and advertising.

But behind this culture there is often a Hidden culture. This is a set of values and behaviors that, in some cases, is very different from those seen by the outside world.

I spent several years working for an international FMCG (Fast-moving Consumer Goods) company whose Formal culture was, "This is a place where everyone can bring their imagination to the office and put it to work. We reward initiative and innovative thinking."

This admirable philosophy would frequently make an appearance in their head office literature, speeches to the staff, and releases to the media. I expect it was at the heart of any sales pitch made by the HR department to a new recruit.

However, nothing could have been further from the truth.

The reality was to be found in the Hidden culture. This company was frightened of innovation and used the philosophy of "Risk Management" to stifle and kill any proposal that advocated a break with tradition.

It was a classic fear culture. Most people were more worried about doing something wrong than they were excited by the possibility of doing something right. The penalty for failure was dire—frequently a pink slip. The notion that people were encouraged to try new things was absurd.

Admittedly, this is a fairly extreme example of the dissonance that can exist between Formal and Hidden cultures. But it serves as a good illustration of the problem we might face when making a persuasive presentation to such a company.

Let's imagine we structure our presentation in such a way that it appeals to the values of the Formal culture. We propose they take an initiative and do something that is radically new. It would involve risk but create the possibility of significant long-term rewards.

Such a recommendation will probably be met with approval on the day. The client team will not betray their values in public. In the case of my FMCG client, they would welcome a presentation that was challenging and edgy. But the minute I was out of the room, they'd trash it. The imperatives of their Hidden culture, the one that exists behind closed doors, would force them to abandon such a risky course of action.

So let's imagine that I make a proposal that is highly risk-averse, has no elements of initiative and innovation, and sits comfortably within their current marketing plan.

Perversely, this presentation may not go so well. There is the very real chance that my work will be rejected on the basis it does not conform to the company's Formal cultural values.

However, once I have left the meeting, it is quite possible that this proposal will be favorably reviewed by the client team. In private, they will acknowledge that it delivers for their organization even if it seems at odds with its public image. Later, they might ask me to make some superficial changes to bring it more in line with their Formal culture.

I'm not suggesting that, when preparing a presentation, you should ignore either the Formal or the Hidden culture. I'm saying it is absolutely vital that you acknowledge both.

Let's go back to my FMCG example one last time.

If the purpose of my presentation is to persuade them to take an innovative course of action, I must be aware of the forces in the room that will resist such a proposal. I need to know that there is a high quotient of Green quadrant safekeeping in any response I'm likely to receive. I need to know that while the Formal culture is encouraging me, the Hidden culture will be my undoing.

Armed with that knowledge, I can build a presentation around the necessary reassurances.

If my initiative is presented within a framework of risk reduction, fallback positions, rigorous testing and research, the study of market precedents all expressed in terms that respect the traditions of the company, then we may see a different outcome. If an innovative proposal can be made to appear relatively safe, then the Formal culture will give me permission to proceed.

So how do we explore a Hidden culture?

This is where getting to know people outside of their working environment can really pay dividends. (There'd be fewer golf courses in the world if this were not the case.)

The only way to infiltrate a Hidden culture is to ask people what it is really like to work in their organization. Or talk to people who used to work there.
In my experience, one of the greatest frustrations of corporate life is to have your plans thwarted by the cultural conflicts within the company. It's a common reason why people choose to leave and go elsewhere. And usually they are happy to talk about it.

So, ask them.

Context

Cultural forces, whether they are Formal or Hidden, tend to prevail over long periods of time. Companies change and evolve slowly. If you were to investigate the corporate giants that rule our world today, you'd find that their cultures are much the same as they were a decade ago. Large corporations talk a lot about dynamism, agility, flexibility, and speed to market, especially when a new management team takes over. But transformation remains a slow and hesitant process.

However, there are forces that will affect your presentation that are changing all the time. Every day.

We call these forces Context.

Some years ago I was working on a launch campaign for a Procter & Gamble product and flew to Cincinnati to present the budgets for our proposed commercial.
The costs were high but not out of line with the premium product we intended to sell. This was not our first production on the brand and we felt comfortable that our figures would be approved.

When I arrived at the Procter building, an extraordinary scene greeted me. It seemed as if half the staff were standing in the reception area. The place was packed. All eyes were glued on the television monitors that were displaying the company's share price to both staff and visitors. The mood was not good. This was the fateful day when millions of dollars were wiped off the company's books as the value of its shares went into free fall.

Suddenly the context of our meeting had changed.

By the time I reached the conference room, a new agenda dominated the proceedings. Gone was the ebullient attitude of "You've got to spend money to make money!" This may well have been a premium product at a high price, but no one, on this particular day, wanted to recommend funding such an extravagantly expensive campaign.

There was absolutely no connection between the project on which I was working and the disaster that had taken place in the stock market. But we felt the effect nonetheless.

Before making any persuasive presentation, it's imperative that you know the context of the occasion.

What's happening? What forces are affecting the people you are addressing? What is going on in their lives and the life of the company? Any information you can divine will help you adjust your presentation and get on the right wavelength.

Recently, I was due to make a presentation to a team I know well. We have worked together many times over the years and have a relaxed, easy communication. But shortly before our get-together, they were told that their boss had been fired and replaced by an outsider.

This dramatically altered the context of our meeting. The dynamics changed as a new set of concerns entered the room. And that required a different purpose, structure, content, and style of presentation.

So how can we discover the context of our meeting or presentation?

As with culture, a certain amount of detective work is needed. If it's a company you know well, you can ask. If you are meeting people for the first time, you may need to do a little desk research. Fortunately, we have the Internet. That can throw up a surprising amount of useful information. Either way, the more you know, the more persuasive your presentation is going to be.

Stages of Change

The underlying purpose of a persuasive presentation is always the same. We want the audience to change. We want them to do something differently or think about something differently. Either way we want a change of behavior.

When preparing a persuasive presentation we need to remember that change is a process. Don't hope for instant transformation. There are a number of steps or stages that will take our audience from current behavior to the desired behavior.

Think of change as a continuum that extends across five stages.

They are:

1. **Pre-contemplation**
2. **Contemplation**
3. **Preparation**
4. **Action**
5. **Maintenance**

This model, called the Transtheoretical Model of Change, was developed by James Prochaska and Charles DiClemente. They were psychologists working in the area of health and addictive behavior. They were particularly interested in the habit of smoking, which serves as a good illustration of their theory.

1 pre-contemplation

2 contemplation

3 preparation

4 action

5 maintenance

Let's imagine that I am a smoker and you would like to persuade me to quit.

I believe that lung cancer is hereditary. We either have a genetic predisposition for it or we don't. This willfully ignorant theory is backed up by the fact that I know quite a few people who have smoked all their lives and the worst symptom they've developed is a cough in the morning. In fact my father was a smoker and it didn't kill him.

Your response to this is to try to sell me nicotine patches. My response
is to show no interest in what you are saying or selling.

Why? I'm in the Pre-contemplative stage.

I'm not even thinking about giving up my cigarettes. I may be in denial of the dangers
or I may genuinely not believe that I am at risk. It doesn't matter. Your argument is
falling on deaf ears.

However, over the next months or years I may move into the next stage of change: Contemplation.

The various TV campaigns, posters in doctors' waiting rooms, leaflets at my children's
school, articles in newspapers, or even the death of someone I know may eventually
get me to reconsider my attitude to smoking.

The government does a lot of work in this area and understands that information is key
in moving people from Stage 1 to Stage 2. Campaigns directed at Pre-contemplatives
are always data-heavy in an attempt to break down their resistance.

In the Contemplation stage I will start to think that I should quit. I don't yet want to
quit but I am starting to see that the cons of smoking outweigh the pros. But I'm still
stuck in the habit and I'll procrastinate and delay the moment when I actually have
to do something. This stage can last a long time as I maintain the balance between the
reasons for wanting to smoke and the reasons for wanting to stop.

When the scales tip in favor of quitting, I'll move into Stage 3: Preparation.

The Preparation stage is when I start making plans to kick the habit. I'll
start looking at ways of quitting—hypnosis, patches, gum, therapy, cold
turkey. I may read Allen Carr's book on how to stop smoking.

I may also decide when I'm going to bite the bullet. It helps to have a date for which I
can prepare myself. New Year's Eve is a favorite for many people, but the date might
be a birthday or a wedding or some other event where I can have a final splurge before
denying myself the pleasure.

Preparation is usually a shorter stage as it contains a timeline as well as a plan.
We're moving consciously and deliberately toward the next stage.

Stage 4 is Action.

This is when I quit. It's New Year's Day or I have come back from the wedding and I have to deliver on my promise to myself. So I stop. If my preparation has been thorough, I have a high chance of succeeding. But this is also the most vulnerable stage. This is when I could relapse and go backward.

Assuming I manage to stay with the program, I'll reach the final stage.

Stage 5 is Maintenance.

In this phase I have quit smoking, I am a non-smoker and I am fighting to stay that way. If I am sensible, I will have found some positive replacement behavior to help sustain my resolve. Perhaps I've taken up a sport, joined a gym, or found a healthy way to spend the money I am no longer wasting on the killer weed.

So where do you and your nicotine patches fit into this model?

In Stage 1 Pre-contemplation, I have no interest in you at all.
In Stage 2 Contemplation, I'll be listening to what you have to say.
In Stage 3 Preparation, you could make a sale. I'm looking for help and I am open to persuasion.
In Stage 4 Action, you have the potential to be my greatest support.
In Stage 5 Maintenance, you should have passed your use-by date.

There are two important things to note from the Stages of Change Model:
1. If you make your pitch at the wrong stage you will be rejected.
2. You can only move people one stage at a time.

Let's look again at your nicotine patches.
In Stage 1, I'm not buying. Don't waste your time selling to me.
Instead, try and move me to Stage 2 by selling me on the need to quit.
The patches can come later.

In Stage 2, I may not buy but I'll be interested. Try to get me to make a commitment to quit. That will push me toward Stage 3.

In Stage 3, I'm buying. In Stage 4, I'm using. In Stage 5, I'm an ex-client.
(Until I relapse and go back to Stage 3 when you can target me again.)

Recently, we experienced a very good example of the Stages of Change
while working for a magazine company.

The sales force wanted to sell their publications to advertising media buyers. They
had an extremely good presentation that clearly showed they had a higher reach and
a lower rate-card than the competitive magazines.
But take-up was extremely slow.

The reason was that the media buyers were in the Pre-contemplation stage. They weren't
thinking about magazines. They were spending their money on television.

Our client then put together a presentation to move their target from
Stage 1 to Stage 2. They looked at the virtue of magazines in general
against the value of TV. In doing this, they excited the media buyers'
interest in their product.

Later they went back with a presentation that showed how competitive
they were against other magazines. This Stage 3 presentation was a great
success and they started to make sales.

There are three lessons to learn from these examples.

First, before you plan your presentation, know which stage of change your audience has reached.

Then build your argument so that it is appropriate.

Second, only try to move them one stage at a time. Any faster and you'll probably lose them.

Third, allow enough time. If they are in Stage 1, you need to plan for
several presentations before they reach Stage 4.

Claim, Value, Proof

Frequently in business negotiations we might find ourselves talking to a customer or potential new client and want to make claims about the services or product we represent. Usually we will want to make superiority claims and avoid parity with our competitors.

There is a danger in doing this. If we're not careful we will make claims that are of value to us but not to our audience. We'll tell them what we think is good about us without thinking about what they actually want and need from us.

We'll end up impressing ourselves and no one else.

I made this mistake many times during my time in advertising. As creative director of the agency I was always proud of our creative work and the awards we had won at various local and international festivals.

So when talking to a new prospect, I'd always make the claim, "We are a creative agency." And I'd back this up by showing some of the work and referencing the awards we had earned.

It never occurred to me that most of our would-be clients didn't give a damn. Our agency's creative reputation was worth nothing to them. Our reputation didn't sell their product. It made us feel good but did nothing to allay their fears and concerns.

A critical aspect of understanding the "Who" is knowing what claims will actually motivate your audience.

Start by asking this simple question:

"What keeps them awake at night?"

Try to understand what worries them. The better you understand their worries, the better you will understand their needs. And if you understand their needs you can structure your presentation to address those needs.

Then review the claims you would like to make and see if they are of any real value. You can do this by using the "5 Whys." It's an irritatingly simple technique.

5. Know the context

Find out what is happening in the lives of the audience that might affect the way they receive you. Are there any unusual events that are having an impact on the group? What pressures are they feeling?

6. Know your audience's "stage of change"

Know where they are and how far you can take them toward your desired course of action. Usually, you can only move them one stage at a time. If you push too hard you'll lose them. Be realistic about what you can achieve with your presentation and state your purpose accordingly.

7. Know what claims will be relevant to them

Use the Claim, Value, Proof filter to understand what you need to say, what ultimate value it represents and how you can prove it. Don't sell yourself to yourself. Make sure your claims are of value to the listener.

8. Study the psychographics and demographics of the audience

Find out everything you can about them. This will help you fine-tune the presentation and preempt any objections and challenges to your point of view.

We've now tuned into the audience's wavelength and they are open to persuasion. We are ready to transmit and they are ready to receive.

What are we going to say?

The "What" comes next.

3. The What:

What is there to say?
What needs to be said?

Planning

There are five principles that guide Aristotle's rhetorical process.

They are:

1. Invention
2. Arrangement
3. Style
4. Memory
5. Delivery

In this section, the What, we are going to take a close look at Stages 1 and 2. "Invention" is where we identify the central questions of our subject and start to marshal our arguments. "Arrangement" is where we organize the information that supports those arguments to ensure that it is comprehensible and memorable.

We'll look at "Delivery" and "Style" in Chapter 4, the How. Fortunately we can dispense with "Memory" as, these days, most presentations are made with aids and prompts.

Aristotle believed that a great presentation is based on the three principles he described as:

Ethos, Pathos, and Logos.

See opposite for how these principles are related. Ethos is our soul. It's born of our experience, our values, and our character. By establishing these qualities, we can build trust and gain the confidence of our audience.

Pathos is our passion. We must show our passion if we want the audience to share our beliefs. It would be unreasonable to imagine we could capture their hearts with an argument that isn't deeply felt in our own.

Both Ethos and Pathos appeal to the right side, the intuitive side of the brain.

However, Logos is our head—our reasoning and argument. It appeals to the left side of the brain and it is where Invention and Arrangement take place.

Aristotle believed that a persuasive argument must be what Ned Herrmann called a "Whole-Brain Experience"—one that engages our head, heart, and soul. The Planning Model has been designed to ensure we incorporate all three from the outset.

The middle circle—the What—is where we explore Logos. We're going to break it down into

Purpose, Information, Organization, and Support.

We'll get to Ethos and Pathos when we reach the outer ring. For now, look at the diagram on page 63.

Aristotle's three forms of rhetoric

Purpose

How often have you sat in a meeting and asked yourself, "I wonder where this is all going?"

A presentation can be full of interesting information, facts, and statistics, and it can be delivered with clarity and wit, but if, by the end of it, the purpose is not clear then it's all been a waste of time—the speaker's time and the audience's time.

Nobody in the room will know how to think or behave, and any "Call to Action" will fall on deaf and bewildered ears.

Purpose is the DNA of persuasion.

Without a clearly stated purpose, your presentation will devolve into a sharing of ideas and data. No more.

This is acceptable if your intent is merely to inform but not if you want to persuade. So, as presenters, the first thing we need to do is understand the general nature of our purpose.

Do we want to inform, entertain, educate, or persuade?

There is a significant difference between the first three and the last. If we want to inform, entertain, or educate, then our hope is that the audience will absorb, enjoy, and learn what we have to say. Their role is passive. We'll be quite happy with a few nodding heads and smiles of agreement.

But if our intention is to be persuasive, then we want the audience to act on what we say. We want to stimulate a change in behavior. Their role is no longer passive, it's active. Our relationship has become interactive.

To do that, we need to understand our specific purpose. Exactly what behavior do we want to change? What is our desired outcome? There's a simple discipline we can use to clarify and establish what we want to achieve and that is to give our presentation a title, a subject, and a purpose. (We don't have to use them on the day, this is simply to help us plan.)

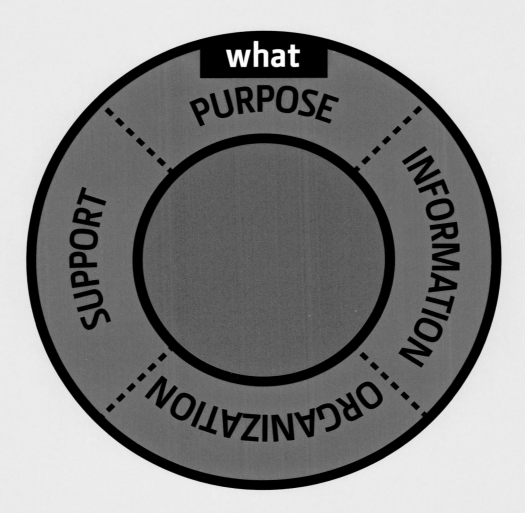

The middle circle of the Planning Model

Let's imagine I am going to argue the case that capital punishment should be abolished in America. My audience is a group of judges, lawyers, and politicians. I want to persuade them to vote against the death penalty in an upcoming debate.

My argument rests on what I consider to be the immorality of state-sanctioned murder. I might title my presentation: "A Death Sentence for our Moral Values." I would describe the subject as: "The moral issues surrounding the incarceration and killing of convicted prisoners."

I would then ensure that the purpose is action-based: "Get the audience to vote against capital punishment."

How is this helpful?

First, it makes sure that we clearly separate our purpose from our subject by being focused and specific.

It's easy to confuse the two. If the purpose becomes too broad or vague it will be lost inside the subject. Remember, in this case, the purpose of my presentation is not to deliver relevant facts and observations on the subject of morality and the death sentence. That is merely the means to an end. The purpose is to get them to act. I want to persuade them to vote against capital punishment. For some of them, that will mean a change of attitude. Being informative is not enough, we need to be persuasive.

Secondly, a clearly stated purpose acts as a good filter. In preparing a presentation we'll usually find more information than we need, or have the time to include.

If we use our purpose as a filter it will be easy to see what information is useful and what we should discard.

Thirdly, knowing our specific purpose will build our commitment to the material and help keep us focused on what needs to be said. This commitment is infectious. The audience will sense the passion we feel for the subject and it will engage their emotions as well as their thoughts.

Lastly, a title is by no means necessary but it can be useful. Titles, if they are good, can act as mnemonics. When your audience thinks back on your presentation, a title can sometimes jog their memory and remind them of the themes that supported the purpose of your talk.

Information

A persuasive presentation is much like a court case.

If we have gained the jury's trust, confidence, and respect they will listen to our opinion. But, understandably, they will reserve the right to disagree and hold an opposing opinion. If we're not careful, the argument will become nothing more than their opinion versus ours. In such a clash, they are unlikely to act on our advice. They'll stick to what they already know and feel. They won't follow our directions and our case will probably fail.

> If we want the jury to support us, we have to prove ("beyond a reasonable doubt"), that our point of view is correct. This may entail proving that their point of view is wrong.

To do that, we need to provide more than an opinion. We need evidence. And this usually comes in the form of information.

If our case is to succeed, we shall provide information that challenges and replaces the information that supports any view that opposes our beliefs and purpose.

> And so it is in any persuasive presentation. We have a saying we like to keep in mind throughout the preparation process:

"Saying it is so doesn't make it so."

We need the facts.

> At the outset, we may face a mountain of information or none at all. If it's the latter, we need to do some serious research. But if we already know too much, we need to do some serious editing and sorting.

Either way, there is only one criterion we need to use when deciding if a piece of information should be included in our presentation.

"Is this relevant to our purpose?"

> Be ruthless in asking this question and remember this principle.

"If it's not working for you, it's working against you."

There have been countless studies of attention span. We laugh at the fact that a goldfish has a memory of only 15 seconds. But research suggests that human beings only concentrate on a given piece of information for just eight seconds! Given this butterfly mentality, we need to do everything we can to capture and hold attention.

The last thing we need is irrelevant information cluttering up the limited brain space of our audience. If something is not actively pushing our argument forward, it's a distraction and must be removed.

This is hard sometimes. Often, in the process of preparing a presentation, we will accumulate a wealth of interesting facts and ideas about our subject. And we become attached to them. We know the audience will find them interesting. And we know we shall enjoy sharing them.

But that is not enough.

We must glue the audience's attention to our purpose from the minute we start speaking to the moment we make our recommendation and suggest the course of action they should take.

Never be tempted to say the words,

"Let me digress for a minute…."

You'll never hear the audience's silent reply which goes something like, "Good, let's relax and stop thinking about what you want us to do for a minute."

If you are tempted to include irrelevant facts and information because you think they are interesting, engaging, and entertaining, then find a way of achieving the same involvement with information that supports your argument. (We'll look at some techniques for doing this in Stage 3, the How.)

So how do we collect information? Start by thinking broadly and then, once you've covered all the ground, start narrowing and focusing your view.

If you are working with a team, you might decide to brainstorm everything you know about the subject under discussion. Get it all up on the wall.

Then move to another wall. Write the purpose of your presentation at the top. Remember to include a brief description of the audience or target in your purpose.

Now transfer only the information that is relevant to your audience and the change in attitude or behavior you'd like them to make. During this process, don't forget that less is more. Audiences are easily overloaded. And if you are dealing with senior management, be mindful of the fact they tend to be generalists. It's the people working for them who deal with the nitty gritty of the details.

These figures will encourage you to focus on the information that most powerfully supports your theme:

25% will be forgotten in 24 hours
50% will be forgotten in 48 hours
80% will be forgotten in 4 days

So be very critical of what you choose to use.

When you've done this, you'll still have a mess of information on the wall. But it will be the right information. To clean up the mess we start looking for themes.

Ideally, your finished presentation will cover three or four themes at most.

Any more and the structure will break down and the audience will think it is listening to a list. And while lists may be easy to follow, they are hard to remember, which makes them useless for the purpose of persuasion.

On the following page is a framework that you can use to help organize your purpose, themes, and information. Write your purpose in the center circle. Be specific about whom you are addressing and what you want to achieve.

Now, give a brief title or heading to each of the themes your presentation will explore and put those in the four boxes around the center.

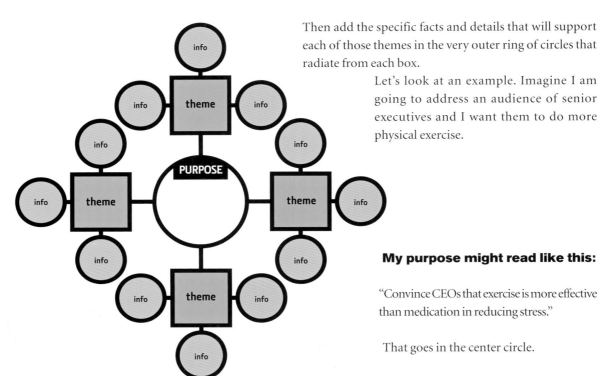

The Purpose, Themes,
Information Framework

Then add the specific facts and details that will support each of those themes in the very outer ring of circles that radiate from each box.

Let's look at an example. Imagine I am going to address an audience of senior executives and I want them to do more physical exercise.

My purpose might read like this:

"Convince CEOs that exercise is more effective than medication in reducing stress."

That goes in the center circle.

I have four themes I will explore. They are: the effect of endorphins on the nervous system, the benefits of sleep regulation, the absence of harmful side effects, and the need for "time out." That's one for each box around the center circle.

Then in the outer circles I'll put in the facts that support each theme. I might have some statistics from endorphin research that quantify the benefits of exercise over the various prescription drugs that are available, so that will go in the one of the circles attached to the endorphin box. And so on.

The illustration opposite shows how my information will be assembled. This simple format will ensure that all of your information is relevant and is collected and organized into a few manageable chunks.

But before we move onto structure, review the information in the outer circles one more time. Wherever you find an abundance of facts and statistics, try to include an example that illustrates the point you are going to make.

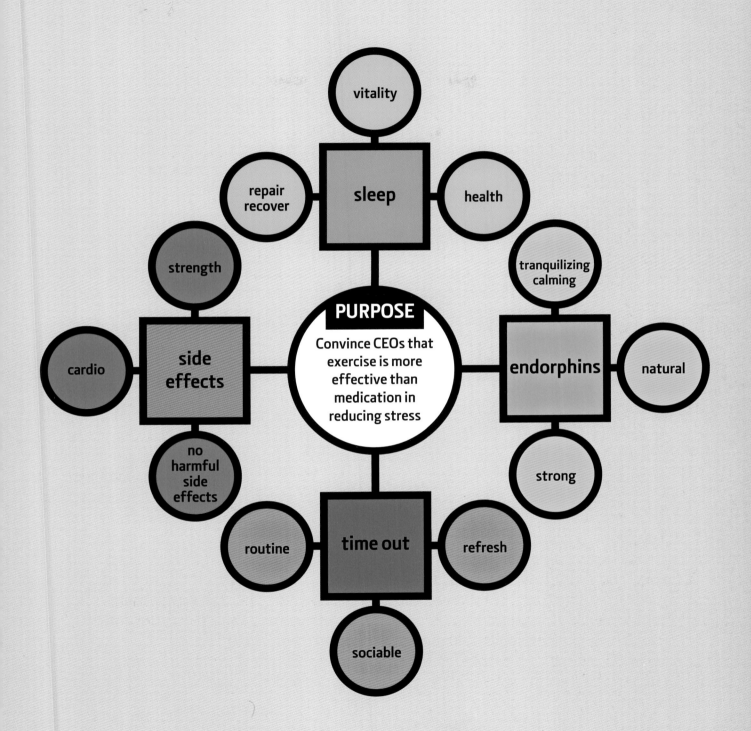

While statistics can be impressive and persuasive, they are often easier to understand and remember if they are accompanied by an example. Numbers, especially to those of us who are not mathematically inclined, can appear abstract. A relevant example can bring statistics back into the real world so that we can really appreciate the message that they contain.

It's been proven in research that we think more deeply about examples and illustrations than we do about numbers. We learn facts and statistics and commit them to memory as accurately as we can. But we explore examples and invest some of our own imagination in them before storing them away. This involvement makes them more powerful and easier to recall.

If I were to tell you that 80,000 people were hurt in road accidents last year, you'd think it was a lot of people. If I said 80,000 people, that's the number who attended the opening ceremony of the Olympics, then you'd "see" just how many people that is. The image would help you experience the number, making it easier to recall.

Once we have established our purpose and collected our information and examples into three or four themes that support it, we're ready to impose a structure that will make the presentation persuasive.

The Organizational Diamond

The mortal enemy of persuasion is confusion. If the audience loses the thread of what you are saying, you will lose the audience.

Structure is how we make sure our listeners stay with us every step of the way—from introduction to final recommendation.

There are four structures commonly used when presenting arguments and information:

Categorical, Problem/Solution, Compare & Contrast, and Sequential.

The Categorical structure is one in which we organize and present our information in categories. It's an effective way of presenting new ideas that don't yet fit a framework. It's not persuasive because it has no underlying intent other than to inform.

The Problem/Solution structure, that is favored by the McKinsey consultancy group, quickly establishes a problem and then proposes a solution that constitutes the company's recommendation.

The Compare & Contrast structure states a problem and then builds a case on the relative merits of the different ways of solving it.

Lastly, the Sequential structure is one that leads the audience along a logical and easy-to-follow path.

The Sequential structure is the one devised by Aristotle for the "Delivery" phase of his rhetorical process.

It's part of what he described as "Deliberative" rhetoric. This is an argument based on deductive logic that establishes a belief and then builds on it, with the intent of changing the audience's opinion.

There are six stages:

1. The Introduction (Exordium)

This is an overview of the presentation that prepares the listeners' minds and helps them compartmentalize the information that will follow.

2. The Narrative (Narratio)

This section explains the current state of affairs. Where we are now and how we got here.

3. The Partition (Divisio)

Here we break down and organize the topics that will be discussed.

4. The Confirmation (Confirmatio)

Here we deliver the arguments that lend credit and authority to our case.

5. The Refutation (Confutatio)

We then anticipate, preempt, and refute any arguments and objections.

6. The Conclusion (Conclusio)

Finally, we make a summary, a call to action, and an emotional appeal to win the hearts as well as the minds of our audience.

These six stages have a very simple underlying structure. A beginning, a middle, and an end. The introduction, the presentation, the summary.

The great virtue of this simple arrangement is that it allows you to repeat yourself without insulting the audience. Repetition is a highly effective way of getting people to remember exactly what you are saying. But if you become noticeably repetitive you'll appear to talk down to your listeners. It's tantamount to saying you think they are stupid and have to hear everything two or three times before they can absorb it.

The beginning, middle, and end structure manages to hide the repetition while taking full advantage of it. We have a slightly different way of saying it:

"Tell 'em what you are going to say, tell 'em what you have to say, tell 'em what you said."

What could be more repetitive? But if it sounds embarrassingly obvious, then think back to our example of the courtroom.

You don't need a law degree or a criminal record to understand the judicial system. There is a plethora of courtroom dramas on our television screens at the moment. In any one of them you'll see this process take place.

The Beginning:

At the start of the case the prosecuting and then the defending counsel will stand before the jury and make an opening statement in which they explain everything they intend to reveal over the course of the trial. They will assert either the innocence or guilt of the defendant and assure the jury that they will back up their opinions and beliefs with incontrovertible evidence. They will tell them what they expect them to do at the end of the trial—acquit or convict.

This is the "tell 'em what you are going to say" phase.

The Middle:

In this, the lengthiest phase of the proceedings, the attorneys will present their evidence and witnesses who can support the assertions they made in their opening speeches.

In this phase, they will go into great detail to prove either the innocence or guilt of the accused.

This is the "tell 'em what you have to say" phase.

The End:

Finally, the attorneys will take it in turns to summarize everything they have said and make the case for, or against, the accused. As with Aristotle's "Conclusio," this final review of the trial will be expressed in highly emotional terms in the hope of swaying the jury by appealing to their feelings as well as their reason. Their final words will be to direct the jury toward a decision.

This is the "tell 'em what you said" phase.

At the end of it all, the jury will have heard the same information three times but the structure will have disguised the repetition while helping them commit the arguments and evidence to memory.

We see the same pattern every night on the television news. It starts with a preview of what we are going to see, then we get the news in detail, and then we get a recap of the major items. We get the news three times.

This may sound simple but it's not obvious to the audience and it's extremely effective.

Let's look at how we can apply these principles to a presentation.

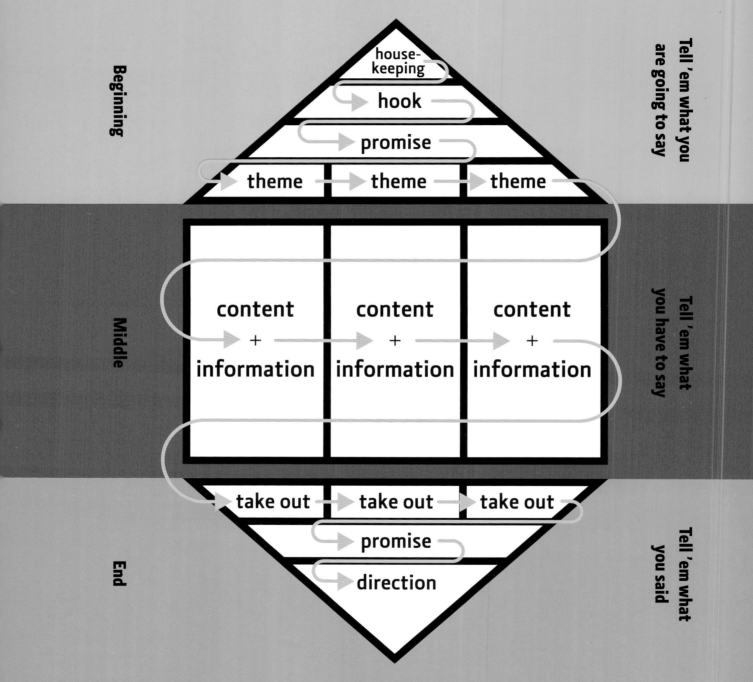

house-
keeping

hook

promise

theme → theme → theme

content
+
information

content
+
information

content
+
information

take out → take out → take out

promise

direction

The Organizational Diamond

The diagram opposite is what we call an **Organizational Diamond**. It's a flowchart.

Once we have established our purpose and arranged our information into three or four manageable themes, we can use the Organizational Diamond to structure the entire presentation.

Let's go through each section and then look at an example of it in action. As you can see, the diamond has three sections: a top, middle, and bottom that correspond to the beginning, middle, and end of our talk.

Let's start at the top.

Section 1: Housekeeping

Housekeeping actually precedes your presentation. In this section you make no reference to the subject you will discuss.

The purpose of housekeeping is to clear the audience's mind of any possible distractions before you start.

These come in many forms and it is particularly important to deal with them if you are the first speaker of the day or your listeners are in an unfamiliar environment. So try to preempt any disruptions by giving them some basic information.

Tell them:

How long you will be speaking before there is a break. Give them the schedule for the day and explain when they'll be able to make telephone calls. Then ask them to switch their phones off.

Let them know if there will be time for questions at the end or if you will be giving out notes.

Explain the eating and drinking arrangements—where and when.

Give them directions to the rest rooms.

In short, tell them anything that will remove distractions and help them to relax and concentrate on your presentation.

Recently, while I was waiting to make a presentation at Unilever, the first speaker explained the escape procedures in case of a fire. This is standard policy at their company. You may find it is a requirement of other large organizations. If something like this needs to be explained, make sure it happens during Housekeeping.

Section 2: **The Hook**

As the name suggests:

The hook is a device for dramatically capturing your audience's attention.

There are many different types of hook and you need to find one that is relevant to your presentation and to your audience. And it needs to be one you feel comfortable using.

Not everyone is good at telling jokes. But humor can be a very effective hook because it connects the speaker with the listener and breaks the icy silence at the start of a presentation.

Some presenters like to use a relevant quote and borrow the authority that comes with a famous name. Dictionary definitions can be effective as can surprising statistics.

I have often found that asking the audience a question is a good way of engaging with them. A show of hands creates a moment of interaction that can break down the barriers that are created by the formality of the situation.

Perhaps the most captivating technique is to stage a stunt. These can range from the subtle to the highly theatrical. There is the story of a Japanese marketing director who was, some years ago, making a presentation to his board with the use of an overhead projector. Before speaking he placed a 100 yen coin onto a clear acetate. The image behind and above him was of a dark circle on a white background.

He asked his fellow directors what they could see. Most of them said the rising sun, Japan's national flag. His reply was a brilliant hook into both his audience and his subject.

"Yes, I expected you would see our flag. That is the way we have tended to see things in this company for many years. But we need to look at things differently. I want you to look at this image and see a globe, a map of the world, because our biggest opportunities lie outside of Japan. This company needs to expand globally. And that is why I am here today."

This gentle but engaging stunt was a wonderful device for capturing his audience's attention, and, at the same time, introducing the purpose of his presentation.

An example from the West perhaps lacks the Japanese flair for subtlety but is nonetheless a powerful demonstration of how a hook can captivate an audience.

In 1987, Kevin Roberts was the president and CEO of Pepsi-Cola in Canada, and about to make a speech to his employees, bottlers, and selected media.

He dressed for the occasion in battle fatigues—a fairly powerful hook in itself—and had a Coca-Cola vending machine wheeled onto the stage behind him. Then, in a display worthy of Jerry Bruckheimer, Roberts pulled a machine gun from behind the lectern, turned, and blasted the machine into smithereens in a pyrotechnic display that left the audience gasping. And cheering.

Before the dust could settle, Roberts said …

"That is what we are going to do to the competition this year."

He then brandished his presentation notes and continued, "And this is the marketing plan that will do it!"

It was an outrageous piece of theater but one that rallied the troops behind him and set the scene perfectly for the talk he was about to give. Thereafter, he was known as Rambo!

My favorite example of a hook is less flamboyant but no less daring. In the 1980s, advertising agency Saatchi & Saatchi in London were pitching for the beleaguered British Rail (BR) business. BR was looking for a better public image because the company stood accused of providing an expensive and inadequate passenger train service for the country's commuters.

Saatchi & Saatchi invited the senior executives and marketing people to visit their offices for a formal presentation of the agency's credentials and recommendations.

When the British Rail team arrived, they found the reception area of the agency was filthy. Ashtrays were overflowing, dirty cups and plates were left on the coffee tables, and the gum-chewing receptionist ignored them while she made a personal telephone call. They were then left to wait for more than 15 minutes.

Understandably, the British Rail team felt insulted and grew restless. At the exact moment they stood up to leave, the doors of the boardroom were thrown open and they were invited into the presentation.

Saatchi & Saatchi's pitch leader then turned the situation on its head.

He explained that the BR team's experience in the reception area was a carefully staged dramatization of how British Rail customers felt about their train service. Passengers expected to wait, to be ignored, and to sit uncomfortably in a messy carriage. It was this negative perception that the agency promised to address through its advertising. Saatchi & Saatchi won the business. Their hook engaged the audience in a drama that brought the theme of the presentation to life. The story also entered advertising folklore and helped build their reputation for brilliant and audacious marketing.

But hooks are not mandatory. It's quite possible to start a presentation without a hook. It may just take a little longer to engage the audience. And no hook is most definitely better than a hook that is irrelevant to the subject you are going to discuss. It would be disastrous if all your audience can remember is an entertaining piece of drama that doesn't help them recall the purpose of your presentation.

Section 3: **The Promise**

This is where your presentation really starts.

Let's imagine that your audience is now sitting comfortably and waiting for you to begin. Their minds are clear of Housekeeping trivia and they may or may not have just enjoyed a joke, a quote, or a stunt that sets the scene for what is to follow.

At this moment they have committed something of real value to you. Their time. In return for that, they are full of hope and expectation. They want to get something out of this experience. They want a return on their investment and, at this point in the proceedings, they'll be wondering what that might be.

So tell them.

Make them a promise. Put their minds at rest by telling them what they will get out of listening to you.

A crude but effective way of doing this is to say, "At the end of this presentation you will…"

> If I was delivering the material of this book in the form of a presentation I might start by saying, "At the end of this talk you will be able to plan, prepare, and deliver a persuasive presentation." (In fact, if you look back to Chapter 1, you'll find I have said exactly that.)

Your promise is essentially the purpose of your meeting expressed in a way that is of value to the audience. By stating it clearly at the start, you will create a funnel through which all of your information and ideas can flow into the minds of your listeners. You are helping them prepare some "mind space" to receive and store your message.

> You are also giving them the reassurance that what you will say is going to be useful to them. If anyone gets up and leaves at this point, let them go. They are in the wrong presentation and you don't need or want their involvement.

Making a promise is the key component in the "tell 'em what you are going to say" phase of the presentation. If it's the right promise the audience will commit their time and attention to you.

You can now build on that.

Sections 4–6: The Themes

Your audience is now listening. You've engaged them and promised them something they want. The next step is to map out the presentation so that they can get an overview of where you are going to take them. Once again, this will help them allocate and prepare the necessary "mind space" to absorb, understand, and retain your information. You're priming them.

You'll remember that, in our section on information gathering, we stressed the need to group all the necessary data, thoughts, and ideas into three or four manageable chunks or themes. (For the purpose of explaining the Organizational Diamond I'm going to assume we have just three themes.)

> This is where we introduce those themes. We don't go into any detail at all.
>
> We give each theme a title and explain that we will be discussing it in depth during the course of the presentation.

Once we've done this, we've reached the end of the beginning.

Let's quickly recap.

We start by clearing their minds with some basic Housekeeping.

> We then have the option of engaging the audience with a hook that breaks the ice and gets them thinking about the subject we are going to discuss.

We then get them to commit to the presentation by stating our purpose in the form of a promise that is of value to them. We show this talk is worth their time and attention.

Lastly, in very basic terms, we tell them about the three themes we intend to cover.

This beginning section should have taken about 10% of the time we are allocated.

> If you look again at the Organizational Diamond on page 74, you'll see how the 80/20 rule applies to persuasive presentations. We spend 10% opening the show, 80% going through our ideas and information in detail, and then 10% wrapping up.

Sections 7–9: The Content

Now they know what is coming, we'll deliver it in great detail. We go through sections 7, 8, and 9 one after another. Using the titles we gave to each theme in our opening, we now present everything we have on each subject.

> This is where we will use props and presentation aids to illustrate the various points and ideas we want to share. We'll explore and exhaust each theme before moving onto the next.

Because this is far and away the lengthiest part of the presentation, it is where you will have to use all of your skills to maintain engagement. The structure of the Organizational Diamond will help. The chance of the audience losing the thread of your argument is remote as you have shown them where you are going to take them.

The most important aspect of these sections is to ensure your delivery is clear and comprehensible. We'll look at visual aids later in this chapter and we'll explore style and technique in Chapter 4, the How.

By the time you have finished going through the content of these sections, your audience will have heard and started to absorb a great deal of information. You have "told 'em what you have to say." You've reached the end of the "middle" and you have no new information to share. But the job is far from finished.

Sections 10–12: **The Take-out**

Information is the means to an end. If your presentation is going to be persuasive, if it's going to effect a change of thinking or behavior, then what matters is how people interpret that information.

Don't leave it to chance. Tell them exactly how you want them to see and understand the facts, figures, ideas, charts, and images you have shared with them.

In sections 10, 11, and 12 you don't just "tell 'em what you said" you also tell them what it means.

Controlling their interpretation of the material is crucial if you want them to agree with you and be persuaded by your argument.

Revisit each theme in turn and succinctly explain what you would like them to take out of the information it contained. Spoon-feed them the message you want them to hear and remember.

Once this has been done, we're ready to bring the presentation to a close.

Section 13: **The Promise Revisited**

At the start of the presentation you made a promise. You said, "At the end of this presentation you will…." Or words to that effect. Now is the time to show that you have delivered on that promise.

So, restate it. Remind them of your promise. Be confident. Show that you believe 100% in what you have been saying. And you believe that they have heard it, understood it, and agree with it.

This is a critical moment. Unless you are met with strong opposition, you now have permission to turn persuasion into action.

Section 14: Direction

The true test of persuasion is whether or not it achieves a change in behavior.

In the closing stages of your presentation you have the opportunity to decide exactly what that change of behavior should be. Again, as with the take-out and interpretation, don't leave it to chance.
Direct your audience.

Tell them how you want them to act and respond to your material. We've all sat through interesting presentations and wondered what we should do at the end of it. Don't let that happen.

Your closing comments must contain precise instructions on what you want the audience to do.

That doesn't mean you have to be heavy-handed. If your argument has been persuasive there will no need to be. But you must be clear in what you want.

This is also the moment where you may have to field some questions and we'll look at some techniques for doing this in the How in Chapter 4. But once you have given direction, the formal part of your presentation has come to a close.
That is the flow of the Organizational Diamond. It's a simple step-by-step process that follows Aristotle's schema. It has a beginning, middle, and end, and it takes the audience on a journey that leads directly to the recommendation you wish to make.

Let's look at an example of it in action.

The diagram opposite is our Diamond for this presentation. We'll use the capital punishment debate again and, for argument's sake, we'll look at it from both sides.

1.
House-
keeping

2. Photo of Sally Ann

3. You will oppose the death penalty

4. Efficacy

5. Morality

6. Fallibility

7.
Case Study
1930–1980

Oklahoma
Brutalization
versus
Deterrent Report

Capital offense
figures
USA 1990

8.
Moral
Feedback

Executioner's
fees

Cruel and
unusual—
Incarceration

Secrecy

9.
Figures of
released
death row
prisoners

70
questionable
executions

DNA testing

10. No Deterrent

11. Immoral

12. Kills innocent
people

13. The death penalty is unacceptable

14. Join our
campaign
by…

We're in Chicago and talking to judges, police officers, lawyers, and social workers. We want them to vote against the death sentence.

Here is the flow:

1. Housekeeping
We take a minute to clear their heads and give them the information about coffee breaks, rest rooms, agenda, telephones, question time, and so on.

2. The Hook
Using my laptop, I project the picture of a happy, ten-year-old girl. And then introduce her:

"I'd like you to meet Sally Ann X. She's ten and lives with her parents in Stockton. Sally Ann has every right to be happy. Her father has just come back from the dead.

"Edward X was about to be the victim of a premeditated killing. On July 19 last year he was due to receive a lethal injection in the state of Illinois. However, two days prior to his violent death, he received a stay of execution and has now been found innocent, acquitted, and released.

"Sally Ann is lucky, but not alone. She is one of several hundred children who have had to wait and wonder if their parents' innocence will protect them from a state-sanctioned murder."

I've made up these names and this story. Unfortunately, however, there really have been cases of wrongful execution. Sally Ann's story should grab the audience's attention, focus them on the subject we are going to discuss and get them emotionally involved.

3. The Promise
"At the end of this presentation, I'm sure that you will all agree with me that the death penalty is unacceptable in this day and age.

"I'm going to discuss three aspects of capital punishment that reveal how inappropriate it is for our legal system…."

4. Theme
"…first we'll look at Efficacy. Is this punishment effective? Does it deter criminals?"

5. Theme

"…secondly, we'll explore Morality. It may or may not be
constitutional but is it morally acceptable?"

6. Theme

"…and lastly we'll look at Fallibility.
Can we be sure that we will not execute an innocent person?"

We've now "told 'em what we are going to tell them." Let's get into the nitty gritty.

7. Content

We look at the information and data we have on the efficacy of capital punishment.
We'll probably cite the 50-year study between 1930 and 1980 that covered five states
in America and proved that the death penalty did not act as a deterrent.

We might also refer to the recent study of Brutalization versus
Deterrence in the state of Oklahoma that suggests that the existence of
capital punishment increases the number of violent crimes.
There is a wealth of data to support this pillar of our argument. We'll
use as much as is necessary to make the point.

8. Content

We now move onto Morality and question the validity of using murder as a punishment
for murder. Isn't there a moral feedback loop that renders this nonsensical?

We might ask why executions are conducted behind closed doors,
usually while we are sleeping. They are never televised. Can we not face
the horror and immorality of our actions?
We might ask why the executioner is paid a special fee. Is that to salve his
conscience for committing an immoral act? We might raise the issue of
the Hippocratic Oath that forbids a doctor to give a lethal injection.
Isn't it immoral as well as unconstitutional to kill someone with such a cruel and
unusual procedure—they are left to wait for years before the sentence is carried
out. They have to face the prolonged fear of their demise in a way that few victims
experience. There is nothing humane about the process.

We might look at religious doctrine on the subject. And so on. There are many
arguments that support the idea that the death penalty is immoral.

9. Content

Lastly, we move on to Fallibility. We'll show photos of the nine prisoners who have been released from death row over the last four years in the state of Illinois alone. Any of these men could have been wrongly executed.

> We'll look at how the legal process failed to protect them and how their lives were saved by the intervention of people from outside of the judicial system.

We'll look at some of the statistics and evidence that surrounds the 70 questionable executions that have taken place since the reintroduction of the death penalty. We'll assess the impact of DNA testing on evidence that was previously incontestable.

> Again, there is plenty of data and information we can use to question the fallibility of the process that leads the convicted to death row.

> As you can see from this brief outline, the middle section of the presentation can be very dense with information. Some of it may be open to differing interpretations. So it is vital that we steer the audience to the conclusions we want them to draw.

We then need to recap briefly and succinctly.

10. The Take-out

We return to the subject of our first theme: Efficacy.

> "Clearly from the data we have reviewed, we can deduce that the death penalty is ineffective. It does not act as a deterrent."

11. The Take-out

Back to our second theme: Morality.

> "You have only to look at our behavior and shame around the death penalty to acknowledge that it is immoral."

12. The Take-out

"The number of men who have been found innocent on death row proves beyond a reasonable doubt that the system is fallible."

13. The Promise Revisited

"And so I am sure you will agree that, given that it doesn't work, is immoral, and is putting innocent lives at risk, capital punishment is not an acceptable sentence…."

14. Direction

"…and for that reason I ask you to join in the campaign to see the death penalty abolished and replaced with a more effective, moral, and safe system of punishing capital crimes. Please write to your state governor etc.…"

Now is the time to say thank you and offer to take any questions.

I've chosen a contentious subject in capital punishment deliberately. There is a strong opposing view to the one we have just given. Let's look quickly at how the Organizational Diamond could handle it.

The diagram on the following page looks at the Diamond for this counterattack.

1. Housekeeping—as before

2. The Hook

Again, I show a picture of a child. This one is not smiling. I introduce her.

"Meet Sally Ann Y. Sally Ann lives with her mother in Jackson. Her father is no longer alive.

"Sally Ann's father was the victim of a shooting incident. The perpetrator was Robert Z, a convicted murderer who was out on parole at the time.

"Would anyone here like to explain to Sally Ann why this was allowed to happen?"

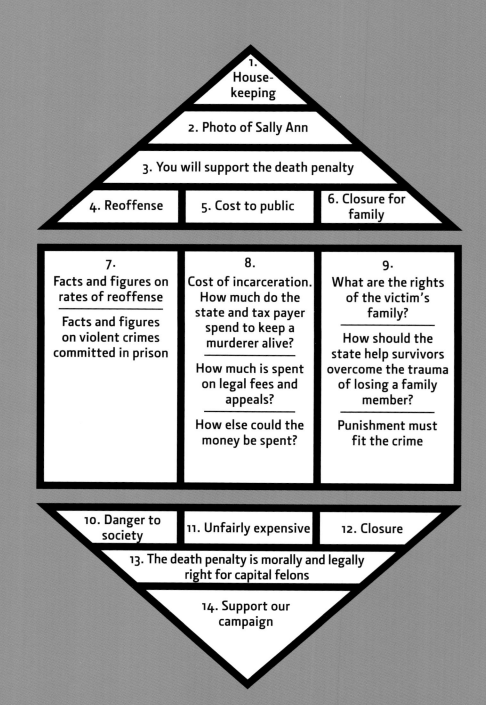

1. House-keeping

2. Photo of Sally Ann

3. You will support the death penalty

4. Reoffense

5. Cost to public

6. Closure for family

7. Facts and figures on rates of reoffense

Facts and figures on violent crimes committed in prison

8. Cost of incarceration. How much do the state and tax payer spend to keep a murderer alive?

How much is spent on legal fees and appeals?

How else could the money be spent?

9. What are the rights of the victim's family?

How should the state help survivors overcome the trauma of losing a family member?

Punishment must fit the crime

10. Danger to society

11. Unfairly expensive

12. Closure

13. The death penalty is morally and legally right for capital felons

14. Support our campaign

3. The Promise

"There is a mood of uncertainty about the death sentence in this state but I am sure that after reviewing the material of this presentation you will have to agree that capital punishment is a regrettable but necessary part of our judicial system."

4. Theme

"There are three issues we need to consider. First, I'd like to look at rates of reoffense. What happens when we release killers back into our society."

5. Theme

"Secondly, I want to look at the unacceptable cost and impracticality of keeping convicted murderers fed and housed for the extent of their natural life."

6. Theme

"And lastly, I want to look at the need for closure that the families of victims experience and which only the death sentence can satisfy."

7. Content

We return to the first theme and look at graphs and statistics that show how often released offenders commit further crimes including murder. We also look at figures that show how prison officers and fellow prisoners are often the subject of attacks by convicted killers.

We build the case the killers are likely to reoffend.

8. Content

We explore the financial implications in depth. How much does it cost the state and the taxpayer to keep a man in jail for life? In the case of a clear conviction, how much should the taxpayer and state pay to fund appeals?

Would not some of that money be better spent on crime prevention and victim support?

9. Content

What are the rights of the victim's family? We might look at some statistics that dramatize the effect of violent crime on the surviving members of the family.

We might question the convicted killer's right to enjoy, albeit in prison, a life that he denied his victim. How can the family attain closure and recover from their trauma when they know the guilty party is still alive and looking forward to parole?

10. The Take-out

"It is too dangerous to society, to prison officers, even to fellow prisoners, to let convicted killers escape capital punishment. The likelihood of reoffense is too high."

11. The Take-out

"The cost of keeping a prisoner in life-long detention is unjustifiably high. As is the cost of appeals. The money could be better spent."

12. The Take-out

"The family of the victim has a right to closure. This isn't simple revenge. It's the ability to move on, knowing that the perpetrator has paid a price that is commensurate with the crime."

13. The Promise Revisited

"Clearly, for the benefit of our society, we must continue to use capital punishment when it is necessary and justified by law."

14. Direction

"I ask you all to join and support our campaign for the retention of the death penalty by writing to your state governor etc...."

Time for Questions

I'm not lobbying for or against capital punishment, but I want to demonstrate that the Organizational Diamond can impose a persuasive structure on either side of any argument.

It has two other great virtues.

When you've created a Diamond you can stretch or lengthen your presentation without affecting its structure or losing your place in it.

The diamond acts like DNA. It ensures that however big or small you make it, the presentation doesn't mutate and lose its shape and form.

Secondly, with practice, it's quick to use and is very helpful with impromptu presentations.

See how quickly you can write a presentation on the following subjects by doing a very basic Diamond. Use just two themes in each.

1. The advantages of using solar power as opposed to the national grid.
2. The advantages of swimming as exercise over going to the gym.
3. The advantages of eating fruit over snack food.

Throughout the examples in this chapter I've stuck to the three themes approach.

Three is a magical number. The presentation as a whole breaks down into three acts, as do most great stories and nearly all Hollywood films. You could say life itself is something of a three-act play.

But there will be times when the complexity of your argument requires four themes. On rare occasions it may require five. But avoid that if you can. Once you have more than four chunks of information, you are overloading your audience and straining their attention.

The best way of maintaining and extending your listeners' attention span is to use the appropriate visual aids. And if a picture really is worth a thousand words, we'd better make sure it's the right picture.

Visual Aids

The most important visual aid in the room is you.

The audience didn't come to read your charts or look at your whiteboard. They are there because they want an interactive piece of theater that gives them the ideas and information they need. You are the star of that show and you must make sure that you are not upstaged by your props.

Visual support is just that—support. It's only there to help you. If it could replace you then you might as well cancel the meeting and send your audience an e-mail with the various attachments you would have shown them.

The 80/20 rules applies here. You need 80% of their time and attention and you can let your support material occupy the remaining 20%. No more. If your visual aids become too dominant, the audience will detach themselves from you and you'll lose rapport and control.

That said, I can't overstate the importance of having the right visual support.

We absorb information through our sensory experience—auditory, visual, and kinesthetic. About 40% comes in through our ears, 40% through our eyes and 20% through our body. So if we want to create a whole-brain learning experience for our listeners, we have to provide relevant visual stimulus.

I stress "relevant" because, as with all forms of information, if it's not working for you it's working against you.

However, the appropriate visual material can achieve two important ends—clarification and retention.

Pictures help us visualize abstract ideas by illustrating the points we want to make. Ideas that are hard to capture in words are often better communicated in images. And images stick in the mind. Visual support not only explains, it helps the audience remember what you are saying.

The chart on the following page looks at the effect visual support has on extending the recall of a presentation over a three-day period.

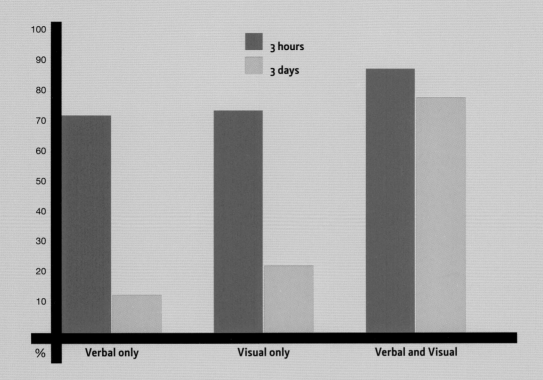

This bar chart tells an interesting story. Imagine you are making a presentation to a group and they plan to reconvene to consider your proposal. If they meet immediately after your talk ends, then you are on pretty safe ground. With or without good visual support, they are going to remember at least 70% of what you said. (With visual support they'd remember 85%.) But if their schedules force them to delay for three days, you have a problem. With inadequate visuals, only 10% of your presentation will have lodged itself in their memories. Not much chance of their following your directions.

The message is clear. If you have the opportunity to use visuals, use them.

But beware of "Death by PowerPoint."

PowerPoint

PowerPoint has become the default medium for visual presentations. I don't know the exact statistic but it seems to me that over 90% of the presentations I attend are made by laptop computer using PowerPoint.

And while it's a wonderful tool, it's dangerous. PowerPoint is an intuitive application and quite easy to use. But it doesn't come with instructions on how best to use it. It's nothing more than a medium. You have to construct the message it sends.

So let's establish the rules.

Here are the ten commandments for using PowerPoint. Write them in stone.

1. Only one idea on each page

If you put more than one idea on a page, your audience will read ahead of you. People can think 2 to 3 times faster than you can speak. Unless you control their attention you will soon be far behind them. While you are carefully explaining your first point, they will be struggling to work out what the rest of the page is going to tell them. They certainly won't be listening to you.

Only one idea on each page

Give each page a title

Abbreviate

Be ruthlessly relevant

Use full sentences for quotes and statements

Build, don't reveal

Aesthetic consistency

Use icons and images

Avoid dynamic typography

Have a Plan B

2. Give each page a title

Introduce each page by telling them what you intend them to take out of it. ("Tell 'em what you're going to tell 'em.") A title is a good way of introducing your message and helping them remember it.

3. Abbreviate

Don't write whole sentences; it only encourages the audience to read and not listen. Instead use bullet points that act as springboards for the points you want to make. Remember the 6×6 rule. No more than six lines on a page, no more than six words in a line.

4. Be ruthlessly relevant

Only include relevant information. It's not what you know, it's what they need to know that matters. Spreadsheets are best avoided because they contain a complex mass of information, much of which will be a distraction from the message you are trying to communicate. Better to extract the relevant figures. But be careful. It's good to round out statistics to make them easier to remember but always ensure that you are accurate. One bad number can, if revealed by a particularly zealous member of your audience, destroy your credibility. And don't load your argument by only including numbers that support it. The audience will smell a rat and think you are trying to deceive them. Use numbers in a fair context. Don't hide the facts that challenge you. Deal with them.

5. Use full sentences for quotes and statements

If you are going to use a quote or a statement, write it out in full. But make a decision. Either invite the audience to read it and then allow the necessary time. Or tell them you are going to read it to them. Don't just start reading and hope that your reading speed matches theirs. It doesn't. They are faster. You will only irritate and distract them if your voice becomes an echo of what they have just read for themselves.

With quotes and statements it's still a good idea to give a title to the page because it directs their interpretation. And remember to cite the source, as this will reinforce the authority of the message.

6. Build, don't reveal

If you have multiple points to make on a single subject or idea, the build function in PowerPoint can be very useful. Each click of the mouse brings up another line and stops your listeners racing ahead of you. It's a far superior technique to using an acetate projector and blacking out your points under a piece of paper and then revealing them as you progress. I always found that intensely frustrating, and expended most of my concentration in wondering what was hidden from view.

7. Aesthetic consistency

You don't have to be a graphic artist to observe some simple design rules when preparing your presentation. There are two that really matter—avoid clutter, and be consistent.

> Use a simple format for your PowerPoint presentation. Try to have no more than two type sizes and two fonts: one for headings, one for text. Keep the number of colors to a minimum, and use them consistently. Ideally, your typography should be contained in the same grid, using the same colors, on every page. Have a designated area where pictures will appear.

Consistency achieves two things. It minimizes distraction and it suggests that you are completely in control of your material.

8. Use icons and images

Words are not images. Often we pretend they are by enlarging them dramatically or giving them unexpected colors. But that doesn't achieve very much. The two remain distinctly different experiences. When we see a picture of a cat, our mind does not experience the letters C, A, T. Unlike words, images are immediate. They may require interpretation but, except in deliberately obscure cases, they don't require identification. The meaning of a picture strikes us instantly, and that is why imagery is so powerful and useful in a presentation.

> These days it's easy to import visuals into a PowerPoint presentation. JPEGs and MPEGs can be easily accessed from within the program. But beware of clichés. Google's image search is a wonderful source of cartoons, drawings, and photos that are frequently free. But they are overused. I don't know how many times I've seen the X-ray of Homer Simpson's brain. And I expect the same staleness will reach film clips as YouTube becomes more prevalent.

9. Avoid dynamic typography

The curse of PowerPoint is that it tempts us to show off. I've sat through many presentations where words have appeared on the screen in the strangest ways. A favorite is for titles to zoom in from either left or right of screen. Why? What does this achieve? It's an irrelevant moment of drama and about as helpful as putting a whoopee cushion into a Shakespearean play. Certainly you'd notice it. But what does it add? Nothing. The only time it might be relevant is if the title was talking about movement or speed. That doesn't happen very often. In the film industry they have a saying: "The best editing is never noticed." Good editing just does its job, which is to keep you involved with the story. The same could be said of typography in a presentation.

10. Have a Plan B

As useful as PowerPoint may be, it's technology. That means it can fail. Laptops, overhead projectors, software glitches—these are frequently the landmines that destroy the path of a good presentation.

A couple of years ago I made a presentation in the boardroom of an electronics company that had a product line of presentation equipment. Even they couldn't get the system going once it had crashed.

You need to go with back-up.

If you have built your presentation in PowerPoint take a hard-copy printout of the key pages. If disaster befalls you, this can work as a handout. It's not ideal because people may race ahead of you. But, quite literally, it's better than nothing. Always take your presentation on a separate USB hard drive. If it's the laptop at fault, you can quickly download your work to another one.

Best of all, check the equipment before the presentation. The day before if possible. If it seems unreliable, you'll have time to switch to one of the presenters' loyal friends: the flipchart or whiteboard.

Most of the rules that apply to PowerPoint apply to them as well. But there are a few specific issues we should address.

Flipcharts and Whiteboards

The inherent advantage of flipcharts and whiteboards is that they give a dynamic role to the presenter.

You create the charts in front of the audience's eyes. This gives you control of pace and content. It also adds a human touch that is lacking from laptop presentations.

There are a few things to watch out for.

1. Flipcharts and whiteboards don't work well in large spaces. Be careful where you place them and make sure you have enough elevation for people at the back of the room to be able to read them and not just see them.

2. Be careful with colors. Some don't read well under artificial light. Red particularly can disappear as will most light colors. And always take your own pens. The ones that have been left for you on the board don't work. That's why they have been left there.

3. Make sure your writing is legible and large enough to be read by the entire audience. Capital letters work best. They tend to be clearer and force you to abandon your normal scrawl.

Lastly, and this only applies to flipcharts, if you are going to attempt a complex drawing or chart in front of a live audience, cheat. Prepare that page first by drawing the image in a fine pencil line. Then you can just trace over it. Apart from giving you the panache of a Parisian street artist, it will ensure that the chart is comprehensible.

Flipcharts do have one unique advantage over other media. They create a working record of the meeting. You can pull them off the pad, stick them on the wall and invite contributions from the audience that can then be transcribed later. Some sophisticated whiteboards have a photocopying function. But let's not forget that photocopiers are technology. They are famous for breaking down.

Many of the charts you prepare will contain a visual representation of numerical data, trends, demographics, and so on.

There are different standard formats that have strengths and weaknesses in helping you do this.

Data Charts

There are five basic charts. They are easy to draw, but I have to admit, PowerPoint does an excellent job of rendering these. They are:

The Pie Chart
The Bar Chart
The Graph
The Dot Correlation
The Quadrant Matrix

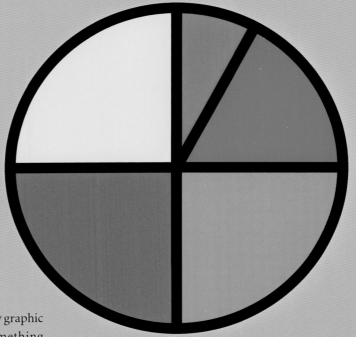

Pie Charts

Pie charts are easy to read and give a very graphic depiction of how the totality of something is divided. They are easy to color and give an immediate sense of how the proportions are shared within the whole. For example, if you wanted to look at the overall food consumption of a nation, you could use a pie chart to display the proportion of meat to fish to grain to vegetables, and so on.

Where pie charts are less effective is in making direct comparisons or displaying two subjects side by side. They can then become confusing.

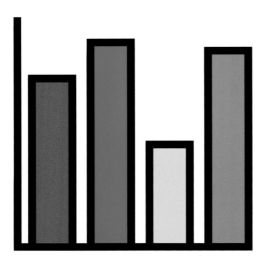

Bar Charts

Bar charts are a simple and instant way of ranking items against one another. They work on two axes. One displays the different items and the other displays the magnitude you intend to measure and display. There is no rule as to which axis is used for which and so the bars can run vertically or horizontally. If there is a protocol, it would be that time is usually on the horizontal axis.

Graphs

Line graphs that are drawn against an x and y axis are probably the most common format for displaying data. They are effective in showing fluctuations, trends, and time-related events. If you want to show a continuous process of change, a line graph is the solution. They are particularly effective in showing the direction of change. The plummeting red line has become an icon of impending business disaster.

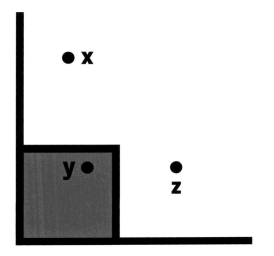

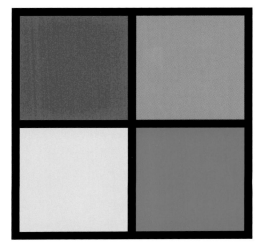

Dot Correlations

Dot correlation charts are often used in financial presentations as they display the comparative performance between two variables. If we were questioning a possible investment on the basis of risk versus return, we'd plot the figures on a dot correlation chart to see where we stood.

Quadrant Matrix

The Quadrant matrix is very helpful if you need to display an analysis of how two variables can interact. For example, in a Brand Belief matrix, one axis might extend from High to Low Belief while the other would chart High to Low Usage. This enables us to reduce **behavior** to just four quadrants and plot any consumer activity within these definitions.

There are many other standard formats for displaying information and data. Triangles convey the combination of three themes. Pyramids are good at describing a hierarchy (as used by psychologist Abraham Maslow to represent the hierarchy of human needs). Clock graphs, rather obviously, convey time and duration. Intersecting circles capture common ground (as in Ethos, Pathos, and Logos). Stars are good for a five-point analysis. Scales can express balance and dominance.

Only one rule applies to all of these devices and it is this:

Images must be communicative not decorative.

It's true that graphs can be visually stimulating, colorful, and a welcome break from a relentless stream of words, but their primary role is to illustrate what you are saying and not just "pretty up" the presentation.

Lastly, bearing in mind our tactile and kinesthetic learning abilities, you might want to take three-dimensional illustrations of what you are saying. It would be hard to imagine an architectural presentation without a model. An anatomy presentation is easier to comprehend with a skeleton on hand. The third dimension helps further stimulate a whole-brain experience.

However, when you introduce this sort of device you must call a temporary halt to your presentation. Don't fight for attention against something the audience can hold in their hands. You'll lose.

Summary and Action Points

The second circle of the Planning Model contains the second process we need to follow when we start work on a presentation.

If you cover these four topics carefully, you'll ensure that you'll use the purpose of your presentation to select the right information. You'll organize it in a way that is comprehensible, memorable, and supported by the right visual aids.

1. Before you start working out what you are going to put into the presentation, work out what you want them to take out of it and why. What change do you want to effect in the hearts and minds of your audience? What is your purpose?

2. Use your purpose as a filter to help you gather the right information and discard anything that is not necessary. Then collect that information into usable chunks and themes.

3. Use the Organizational Diamond to impose a structure on your information that makes it easy to follow, easy to understand, and easy to remember. The Diamond will take your audience on a journey from the unknown to the known and leave them certain of what you require them to do.

4. Develop visual support that clearly illustrates the themes of your presentation. It must support and not obscure what you are trying to say. While it must be stimulating, it must be edifying.

4. The How:

How do we tell 'em?

The Line

The Washington columnist Roscoe Drummond once said, "The mind is a wonderful thing. It starts working the minute you are born and never stops until you stand up and speak in public."

We all know this experience.

I've sat in many meetings and waited for my turn to speak. Usually, as the speaker in front of me starts to wind up his presentation, I'm tempted to disengage from whatever he or she is saying and start to review my notes and mentally rehearse my opening remarks. At this point, I'm feeling slightly nervous. My hands will be sticky, my heart beating with a thump, and my breathing will be faster and shallow.

Believe it or not, this is a good thing. This is my body preparing me for the performance I'm about to deliver. If I'm going to be at the top of my game, I need the adrenalin to fire me up.

But we often confuse fear and excitement. Physiologically, they are very similar—the sweaty palms, the pounding heart, the fast breathing, the butterflies. Some people thrive on these sensations and spend a lifetime pursuing extreme sports and adventures. And some of us interpret these feelings as a warning of imminent danger and recoil accordingly.

Anxiety is one of the main obstacles in the path of a good presentation, so let's look at it in some depth.

When we stand up to speak, we separate ourselves from the audience and, metaphorically speaking, cross "the line." This line divides us from them. It's invisible, but we feel it acutely. Suddenly, we are no longer part of the group. We are facing the group. And by "facing," I mean we are confronting them. As we first look at them, these former friends and colleagues are suddenly sitting in judgment of us.

What do we fear?

We're afraid of performing poorly, looking foolish, and failing to win the audience over to our point of view. And we may fear that our material is not up to the job.

These are significant pressures and they are made all the more intense by the fact that we are standing in a spotlight and bearing the silent scrutiny of our judges. Throughout the proceedings we may get little feedback and not know how well we are doing. In that bubble of isolation, we'll hear only our own voice and be intensely aware of anything we say that feels wrong or inappropriate.

There can be no doubt, public speaking is a confrontational situation. That is why so many people are terrified of it.

But, as with so many things in life, the prospect is far worse than the reality, which is perfectly manageable. We just need a combination of attitude and technique. And practice.

The ancient Greeks believed in the power of nervousness. They believed that by facing these fears a speaker is forced to make sure the material has been properly prepared. He or she will also be encouraged to engage and connect with the audience to break down the perceived barrier that separates speaker from listener.

So before we look at how we deliver our carefully planned presentation, let's look at some techniques for crossing "the line."

Attitude

You can release a lot of pressure if you stop relying on yourself and start relying on your material.

That is why this book has placed so much emphasis on collecting the right information and organizing it in a structure that will support you.

Many presenters fear getting lost in the middle of their talk. They have a nightmare image of themselves standing in front of the audience with a blank mind and no idea of what to say next. They imagine the shame and embarrassment of "losing it."

This can even happen to professional performers. Laurence Olivier suffered notoriously from stage fright and considered abandoning his career in the theater because of it. I once met a pianist who, before his first solo live television performance, told the camera crew and producer that he suffered from epilepsy. He didn't. But he had convinced himself that if he "lost it" on air and his performance went to pieces, he could feign an attack of epilepsy and emerge with greater dignity than if he had merely succumbed to nerves. Fortunately, he played very well and never resorted to this drastic tactic.

The Organizational Diamond can protect you from such delusional thoughts and behavior. The structure will make sure that you don't lose your place in the presentation or forget the flow of your argument. If you are distracted, you can easily pick up the thread and continue.

Knowing this can be a great source of confidence and security. You'll find that once you place your trust in the preparation phase, the performance itself can be enjoyable. How you view the audience is also important. If you view them as superior, you will feel inferior. Simple as that. Winston Churchill, one of history's most brilliant public speakers, used to imagine his audience naked. He found it to be a great leveler.

Always remember that every member of the audience would be experiencing the same feelings of nervousness and self-doubt if they were in your position. Unless the meeting is a blatantly hostile occasion, the audience will have feelings of sympathy for you and want you to do well. They are more likely to be for you than against you. Although you are unquestionably the star of the show, the best possible attitude is to regard yourself as a conduit. The presentation will flow through you.

You are the delivery mechanism for something you have polished to perfection.

The best attitude to sustain you in front of an audience is pride. And that comes from knowing you have prepared well for them.

Technique

It's essential to relax.

If the audience senses you are stressed, they will interpret that as a lack of confidence. This will then reduce their willingness to believe what you are saying.

If you are, by nature, prone to nervousness, then you need to use some relaxation exercises before you go to the meeting. There are three that seem particularly helpful with stage fright: visualization, breathing, and meditation. You need to set aside some time to calm your nervous system. Ten minutes of controlled breathing is surprisingly therapeutic. It oxygenates the system and relaxes tension in the muscles, particularly those in the chest that can affect your voice.

Positive visualization is a good way of reprogramming your fears. Spend just ten minutes with your eyes closed and rehearse the presentation. Imagine how you would like to deliver your material. Visualize it very clearly. Let yourself be inspired by an image of you doing it well and not inhibited by a fear of doing it badly.

Meditation, if you have learned a technique, is a very effective way of finding a calm center that nervousness doesn't reach. If you have this skill, then use it.

Also, before the meeting, find somewhere you can warm up your voice. Practice your opening aloud. Practice speaking slowly and clearly, and control your volume and pitch. Get comfortable with your voice. It will be the most important instrument in the room.

> Once you are at the venue, it helps to interact with the audience if you don't already know them. This breaks down barriers and will reassure you that they want to listen to what you have to say. Even small talk before the meeting starts will help put you at ease because it establishes a connection.
>
> Once you cross "the line" there will be a moment of realization. The waiting is over, you are now up in front of them and they are watching and waiting. Two things can help take the edge off this moment.

First, control the way you are introduced. If one of your team has been assigned to explain your presence or if there is an emcee, be sure to supply the script. Make sure your audience knows what you want them to know about you so that you can engineer their first impressions and create the right expectations. It's a disaster if you have to start your talk with them misinformed or with an apology and a second introduction that you have to give yourself. You need the stage to be properly set for you so that you feel comfortable.

> Second, if the first moment seems intense, stay with it. Relax into it. Don't rush. If you need something to do while you collect your thoughts, smile and take a sip of water. (Or ask for some water.) The rush of adrenalin will pass. Just give it a second or two.

This is where Housekeeping and a Hook can really help you. Housekeeping will give you the chance to adjust your voice to the size of the room and number of people. But if a previous speaker has attended to any Housekeeping, your Hook will allow you to make contact with the audience and build a rapport that you will find reassuring—particularly if the Hook requires a response from the audience or gets them smiling, nodding, or laughing.

Remember to talk slowly and clearly. It gives you time to think and it makes you look confident. And confidence is infectious. If you look it, they will feel it.

The last thing I'll say about confidence is this: the single most powerful antidote to anxiety is rehearsal.

Rehearsal removes our most insidious fear: fear of the unknown. Rehearsal gives you a real-time experience of the presentation and allows you to see where the dangers lie. Frequently in rehearsal you will find yourself changing the presentation to allow for miscalculations in the time required. Usually, we allow too little time. Better to know that and make an adjustment before you find yourself in front of an audience making an apology.

Sometimes you'll work with a colleague who refuses to do a rehearsal. The usual excuse is, "I do it better on the day. I need to be fresh." This is garbage. They are afraid of the rehearsal because they find it difficult to transform themselves into their presenter style and personality in front of people who know them well. Insist. Accept no excuses. I've had my own presentations ruined by colleagues who have run over their time slot simply because they didn't rehearse. Don't let it happen.

It's important to take these psychological preparations seriously. Your state of mind and sense of self-control is immensely important in the process of delivering a persuasive presentation. Research has shown that your audience will absorb your message through three means of communication: your words, your voice, and your appearance.

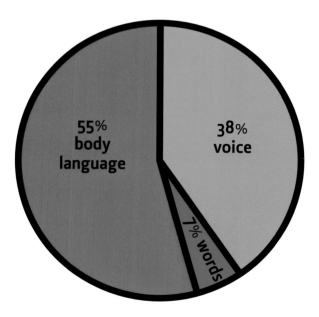

55%
body
language

38%
voice

7% words

Metaphors work in much the same way. They can transpose our subject into a different image world that illustrates the theme or message and brings it more vividly to life.

War and sports seem to be favorite metaphors for the highly competitive world of business. We often hear talk of "slam dunk" successes, "killing" the competition, and so on.

Just about any activity can be used as a metaphor for some other activity if they share some common values. Recently, I was watching a documentary about the World Ultimate Fighting Competition—a brutal mix of boxing, wrestling, and martial arts. The winner was known as "The Smashing Machine." The inhuman world of machinery was a wonderful metaphor for the mindless, heartless, insensate behavior of the champion. Once he had pinned his opponent to the floor, he showed no thought or feeling as his arms mechanically pummeled him.

Metaphors and analogies are also very good at making the abstract more concrete. One of my favorite examples is about need and was a popular button during the women's movement of the late sixties and seventies:

"A woman needs a man like a fish needs a bicycle."

The absurdity of the imagery underscores the message. (How absurd to think a woman would need a man!)

When reviewing your material, keep an eye out for adjectives and adverbs. They are lazy forms of speech because they don't excite the imagination. They simply describe. They qualify. It's best to avoid them.

Whenever possible, if you need to amplify your meaning, it's better to use metaphors and analogies to stimulate the imagination and the senses of your listener.

We also use words to tell stories and a narrative structure is an extremely effective way of engaging an audience and leading them to your point of view. Stories can give wonderful examples of a theory or idea.

Let me tell you a story to show how a story can be helpful.

A while ago, I ran a workshop on creative thinking and tried to explain the creative process. I looked at its five stages and explained how inspiration comes from what Arthur Koestler calls "the intersection of two matrices of thought." I went on to state that this intersection often comes in the form of a random event.

I was confronted with a room full of either blank or bored expressions.

So I told them a story. I explained how Archimedes had been trying to work out the amount of gold in the king's crown without resorting to melting it down, when he had sat in a bath and noticed the water start to overflow the brim. In a flash, he had the answer to the problem. How? Two thoughts had immediately collided or "intersected" in his mind—one thought was about the volume of an irregular-shaped mass and the other was about the displacement of water. "Eureka!"

The story both explains a rather dry theory and brings it to life. As with metaphors, stories can ground abstract ideas in recognizable real-life experience and make them comprehensible.

Most religions use stories as a didactic device for spreading their doctrine. Parables are moral stories that illustrate the beliefs to which that particular religion adheres. The value of the story is not in its narrative but in its meaning.

The parable of the loaves and the fishes in the Bible has all the limited narrative drive of a magician's stage show. But the meaning is about the need to share and the belief that God will provide.

This principle applies to the stories we might use in a persuasive presentation. The story needs to be interesting and entertaining if it is to hold the audience's attention. But, equally important, its meaning needs to be made clear.

The image of Archimedes running naked through the streets shouting "Eureka!" is an amusing anecdote but only relevant or useful because it serves as an example of "intersecting matrices of thought."

So when using stories as examples or illustrations, we need to do three things: explain the purpose of the story, tell the story, and then explain the meaning of the story. Never leave the interpretation of the story open. Always extract and state the meaning and attach it to your purpose.

Humor

Laughter is a great connector.

When we tell a joke or an amusing story, we bring the audience and speaker together in a shared experience. Which is why jokes, as long as they are relevant, make such great hooks at the start of a presentation.

Humor also creates a good mood in the room. It relaxes the audience, puts them in a positive frame of mind and makes them more receptive.
It can also say a lot about you. Wit reveals intelligence in way that doesn't alienate your listeners. It contains a warmth that makes them feel comfortable and not threatened.

Self-deprecating humor is particularly good at breaking down barriers. Human beings like people who don't take themselves too seriously. The audience will feel closer to you if you can see your own failings and foibles and make fun of them. Assuming that is appropriate to the occasion.

Recently, I saw Al Gore make a televised speech on the subject of global warming. His opening comment was, "Good evening. Let me introduce myself. I'm the man who used to be the next President of the United States." The wry tone of his delivery managed to poke gentle fun at the swerve his career had taken and yet, at the same time, establish his credentials for talking on this particular subject.

The language of humor is very engaging. It relies on stories and analogies and stimulates the senses, forcing the audience to think in pictures.

(The exception is puns—we groan at puns because they are merely a play on words and don't use language to fire up the imagination.)

The danger of humor is that it can fall flat. Or backfire. The audience will feel uncomfortable if you make jokes that are inappropriate or not funny. The television show *The Office* is a painful example of a man who thinks he's funny, but he's not.

The experience of watching him is acutely uncomfortable. The brilliance of the performance is that it goes to such an extreme that it does actually become funny. Sadly, in real life that doesn't happen.

> The best way to make sure your humor will add to the presentation is to rehearse it. Only a handful of comedians in the world actually ad-lib their performances. The rest rehearse. They find material that works for them and use it over and over again. That's why it sounds natural.

Again, if you are looking for humorous anecdotes or jokes that may inspire you, the Internet is a good place to start. There are many sites you can search by subject matter to find jokes and anecdotes you can then adapt to your style.

The most important thing is to feel comfortable with the material. If you don't find a joke amusing, your audience won't either. It might be hilarious if told by a comedian but if it doesn't suit your way of talking or your attitude and manner then avoid it. Gentle humor is always better than forced humor.

Your Voice

We talk all day long, so it rarely occurs to us that we need to practice talking. But in a presentation we speak differently. We use a different voice and if we don't practice, we won't use it well.

Some years ago I had to give testimony on behalf of the defense in an important jury trial. I spent some hours in the counsel's chambers rehearsing what I was going to say. We went over the material many times and tried to anticipate any difficult questions that would be posed by the prosecution. By the day of the trial I knew the material inside out and went to the courthouse feeling confident but quite nervous. I had to wait outside the court for two days to give my evidence. By the time I was sworn in, I'd been over my testimony a thousand times in my head.

> But the first few minutes were disastrous. At that point, despite my truthfulness, I'm sure the jury would have found me totally unconvincing.

I had failed to imagine the size of the room. While rehearsing in chambers I had spoken conversationally. Now, I was about 30 feet (10 m) from my audience in a room with high ceilings where my voice floated and wafted ineffectually. I sounded weak and frail. Worse still, I sounded uncertain.

Mercifully, my appearance before the jury came at the end of the day and the trial was adjourned early. I was able to go home where I spent the evening delivering my testimony to the birds in my garden. When I returned next morning, I had developed sufficient projection to reach my audience and sound convincing.

A massive 38% of your communication's credibility comes from the quality of your vocal delivery.

That makes your voice the second most important instrument in the room for getting your audience to believe in you. (We'll get to the most important instrument last.)

Our voice reveals our "Pathos," our passion for the subject. When people listen to our voice they hear our feelings as well as our words. They can measure the depth of our conviction and belief in what we are saying. The more we believe, the more likely they are to believe.

As well as revealing our own feelings, our voice can control theirs. We set the mood and tone of the meeting, we create drama, light and shade, pace, and emphasis, all with our voice.

Imagine your voice has the sophisticated control panel we find on some expensive hi-fi amplifiers. Volume, Tone, EQ, Balance, Loudness, On/Off, and so on. We need to learn how we can adjust these controls to suit the occasion, the room, the audience, and the message.

Volume is our primary control. It's usually the biggest knob on a hi-fi display. By adjusting volume we make sure that everyone in the room can hear us comfortably without straining or leaning forward. That's important. If people are struggling to hear, they can't fully concentrate on what you are saying.

> But volume is also a mood, tone, and relationship control. When we speak loudly we are asserting ourselves. We are stating our authority and raising our pedestal slightly. When we speak more quietly, we draw the audience in and create intimacy and collusion.

> When we speak loudly we are telling them what we think; when we speak quietly we are sharing what we think. Clearly, this creates a different relationship with the audience and one we must consciously manage.

This relationship may change throughout the course of the presentation. While delivering ideas or information that we believe are beyond dispute (or want to be beyond dispute), we may choose to speak with authority—perhaps not loudly, but firmly. Then, when asking the audience to share our interpretation or conclusions, we may want to create a sense of dialog and closeness—we'll speak more quietly. In this way, volume controls the emotional distance between speaker and listener.

Volume can also control levels of attention. I used to work with a CEO who had the habit of speaking quietly at critical moments in his presentations. He knew that once he had captured his audience's attention, he could deepen that attention by lowering his voice and creating a sense of stillness in the room, then everyone had to concentrate more fully on what he was saying. People would never interrupt him at these moments. He always judged it well. Had he gone too far, no one would have been able to hear him at all.

> When reviewing your material for the presentation, identify those areas where you want to speak with authority and those where you want to draw the audience more closely to you. Volume control will help you achieve the relationship you want to develop.

Pitch is a more complex variable and harder to control. It reveals the intensity of our feelings but often does so unconsciously. When we are upset, nervous, or distressed our voice will tend to become shrill. When we calm down, the pitch of our voice will drop. Managing this takes some practice. If we want to appear calm and confident we need to keep our voice centered in our diaphragm. If we become nervous, it will creep up into our chest. This gives our voice a slightly constricted sound that the audience will interpret as uncertainty.

Relaxation, calm breathing, and conscious awareness are the keys to controlling pitch. Once you have "centered" your voice, you'll find you can raise it without altering the pitch in a way that might suggest that you are uncomfortable with either the situation or what you are saying.

Pace often escapes our attention. When we are nervous, particularly at the start of a presentation, we tend to speak too quickly. As we calm down, we slow down. Once again, an unconscious vocal mannerism is giving the audience clues as to how we really feel, and so we need to control it.

Once under our control, pace is a useful tool. Speaking quickly can convey excitement. But it can also suggest that this section of the presentation is not meant for profound investigation. We skip over material by speaking quickly.

On the other hand, speaking slowly can suggest that the material under discussion is worthy of a deeper analysis and should be taken very seriously.

Pace allows you to introduce variety—light and shade—into the presentation and avoid a metronomic and boring rhythm. Changes of pace always stimulate attention and involvement.

As with volume and pitch, the issue with pace is one of intent. Once you bring them into consciousness, all three controls allow you to manage the emphasis you place on the thoughts you are expressing.

Winston Churchill was a master of emphasis. His handwritten or typed speaking notes reveal that he arranged the words graphically on the page to prompt him to give the desired emphasis. Some words he underlined, others he wrote in capitals, sometimes he stepped the lines to show how the phrases would flow. (The Library of Congress website has some good examples of how he did this.)

Emphasis is how we embed information in memory. In any presentation there will be more data, thoughts, and ideas than the audience can or wants to remember. Control of emphasis is how you control what they do remember. This comes from your voice as well as from the structure of the presentation.

There is one button on our voice control display that we are hesitant to use. The on/off button. Silence is a very powerful tool.

But we tend to avoid it.

Why? Probably because we are afraid of boring the audience. We think if we are not saying anything, their minds will switch off. They'll stop listening.

The reverse is true.

Silence creates anticipation.

Silence heightens the audience's attention and stimulates involvement.

Jazz trumpeter Miles Davis said that he didn't just play the notes, he played the silence between the notes.

If, at the start of a presentation, you want to establish your authority in the room then say nothing. Stand and wait for the silence to bring the audience to you. Show that you have the confidence to just wait for their attention. Show that you will not be ready until you can see that they are ready.

If, during the course of a presentation, you want them to think deeply about something you have said then give them some silence in which to do it. Hit the "off" button for a second or two. By watching your audience, you'll know when to start again.

Watch any great speaker at work and you'll see them using silence as well as words to control their relationship with the audience.

Lastly, you might want to use some vocal exercises to warm up your voice. Some speakers like to use tongue twisters to get their mouths and lips working.

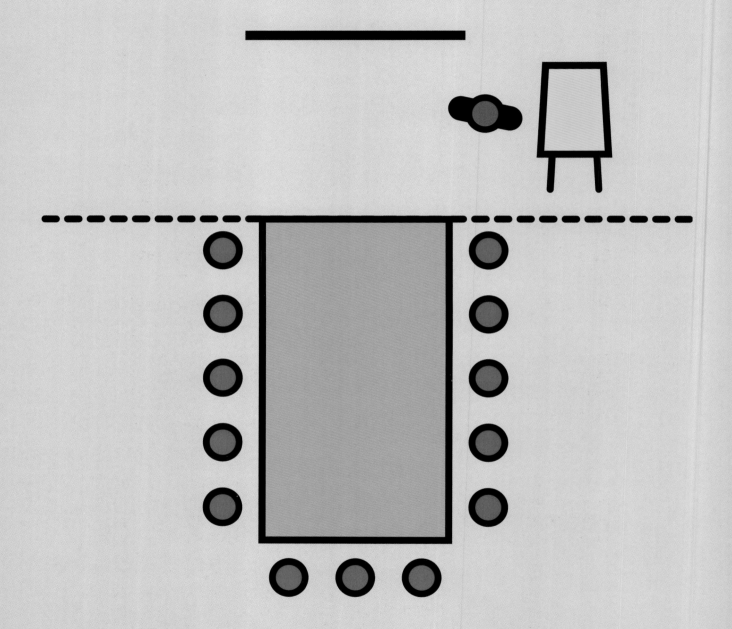

The "Teacher/Facilitator"

Your Place of Power

Where you stand in the room defines your relationship with the audience. The illustrations on the opposite page and the following two pages look at the three most common options.

Let's assume you are delivering your presentation in a room where your listeners are grouped around a boardroom table. At the front of the room you have a flipchart or whiteboard and a screen that displays images from your computer.

In the illustration shown opposite, you stand by the flipchart. You maintain the "Presenter's Triangle." This is the triangle that exists between you, the listener and the pages on which you are writing. It's vitally important that you maintain the triangle because it will help you avoid the cardinal sin of turning your back on the audience.

While in this position, you are the "Teacher/Facilitator." That is your role. You are working with the group to help them develop an understanding you already have.

In the illustration on the following page, you have moved. You are now standing beside and slightly in front of the screen. In this position your role has become that of the "Lecturer." (You may even be behind a lectern.) You are delivering your words of knowledge and wisdom in a less interactive fashion. Your audience's role is more focused on listening and less on making a contribution to the debate. You won't turn your back on them but you may well point to images on the screen.

In the illustration on page 131, you have left the front of the room and are standing beside and close to your audience. You have joined them. In this position you are part of their team—a leader or a "Coach." Your language will probably move from the "I" to the "we" as you work from within the group to get your point across.

There is a further option. Sit down. Physically join the group and end any separation between yourself and your audience. This can be effective. It creates a moment of sharing and intimacy and is good if you don't mind the spontaneous feedback it will encourage.

But a word of warning. Some people, when it's a relatively small group, like to give their entire presentation sitting down. They claim it keeps them closer to their audience, not just physically but emotionally. And it does. But I'm suspicious of this instinct. In many cases I think it's an attempt to avoid the separation anxiety that comes from crossing the line.

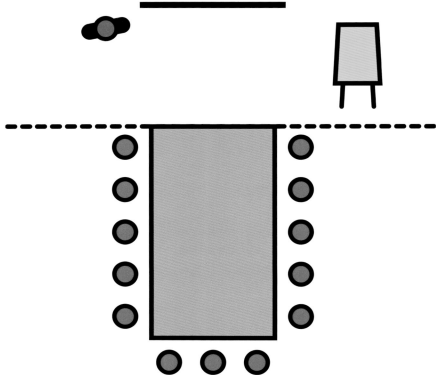

The "Lecturer"

My advice is to stand up and take the position that best suits the role you want to play. Standing focuses the audience on you and lets you command their attention and respect.

Lastly, when moving from one position to another, try not to walk and talk.

Physical movement creates energy in the room. If you are walking from the back of the room to the flipchart at the front, moving from a coaching role to a facilitating role, your audience will wait for you to get there. You don't need to fill the moment with talk to suppress the silence. Use it. It's a moment of anticipation before you resume the presentation.

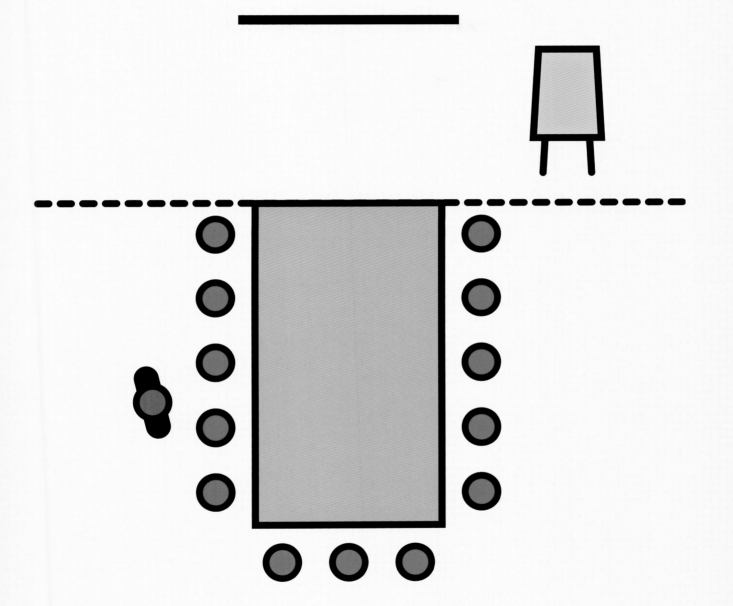

The "Coach"

Gestures

Three questions surround the issue of gesturing in a presentation. Why do we need to? How much should we do? What do we avoid?

Gesturing comes naturally to us. In different countries and in different cultures, varying emphasis is placed on gestures in conversation, from the restrained to the positively flamboyant.

No matter the extent of our gesturing,

it's a human need to underscore what we are saying with some physical movement.

How often have you watched someone making hand gestures while talking on the phone? It serves no communication purpose but it satisfies a fundamental need.

Try giving directions to somewhere without using your hands. Even if you put your hands in your pockets you'll find your head twitching, your shoulders turning or your eyes sliding to one side when you say something like, "Turn left at the lights, go straight, and then turn left again." It's impossible to resist the instinct.

So don't resist it, control it.

Gestures serve many valuable purposes. They enable us to emphasize or enforce a point we are making. They can help us describe a shape or action. They can communicate size—large and small—and speed. They add visual punctuation to what we are saying and can be used for dramatic effect. They can invite or forestall audience participation. Gesturing is very versatile and very eloquent.

The real issue is how much gesturing should we do when making a presentation. The answer depends on three things: You, Your Audience, and Your Environment.

The gestures you make must feel natural or they will look unnatural. If that happens, your audience will feel uncomfortable in much the same way you do. They may also feel your manner is fake and therefore untrustworthy. So rule number one is don't make gestures that don't work for you first, the audience second.

The nature of your audience and the nature of the relationship you want to have with them will also dictate the gestures you can and cannot make.

High gestures tend to be very strong and assertive, whereas low gestures are weaker, less confident, and less emphatic.

Open palms and bent arms embrace the audience and will draw them in and invite questions and contributions. Straight arms will repel them.

The size of the room will affect the size of your gestures. It's a simple relationship. The bigger the room, the bigger the audience, the bigger the gesture needs to be. It's exactly the same principle you'd use with the volume of your voice.

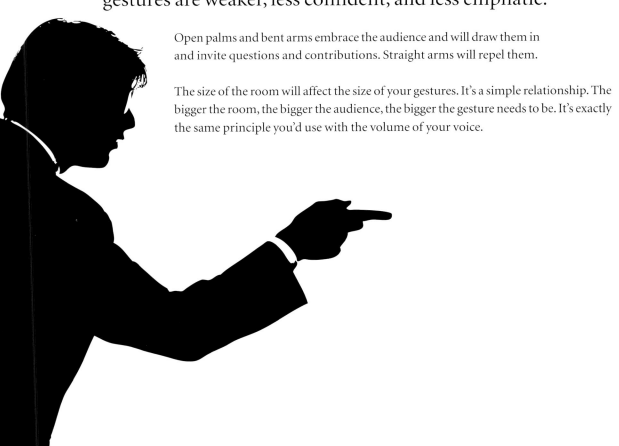

Facial Expressions

Your audience will unconsciously absorb the information your body is sending but spend most of their time looking at your face. They'll be "reading" your face. They'll be wondering how you feel about the material and the presentation and they'll be wondering how you feel about them.

Some people are very facially expressive. They raise both eyebrows to create a question mark, one eyebrow to express doubt, close both eyes and screw up their face to express disbelief, and so on. If that is your style, then fine. It can be very effective and engaging.

But if you are less expressive, remember one thing: Smile when it's appropriate. Treat the audience as a friend. Try not to let your concerns appear on a furrowed brow because it is an invitation for the audience to worry about what you are saying. They will take their cues from you.

Eye Contact

Eye contact is the single most important gesture you can make.

When you look directly at someone, it means you are talking directly to that person. As your intention must be to talk directly to everyone in the room, you must look at them all. That means you need to develop the habit of constantly scanning your audience.

A friend of mine was a successful trial lawyer in the U.S. Over the years, he learned the necessity of using his eyes to connect with all 12 members of the jury. In the opening days of the trial he would look directly at them one after another while he was talking—just a couple of seconds each—and then move on.

As the trial wore on, his intuition would tell him who were the key members and decision-makers behind the closed doors of the jury room. He did this simply by feeling the response to his eye contact. Later, during his summing up, he would appeal to those decision-makers by giving them just an extra beat of time when his eyes met theirs as he was making an important point. He always attributed his success to this ability to communicate through eye contact and, at the same time, gain valuable feedback to his argument and presentation.

Direct eye contact suggests honesty and openness. If you avoid people's eyes it suggests that you have something to hide. You look "shifty."

Practice is the answer. When rehearsing, scan the room in a slow and methodical manner. If you have a live audience, ask them if they all felt included. It's easy to make the mistake of identifying a key decision-maker and then ignoring the rest of the room—particularly if you sense you are getting a positive response.

Some years ago, I missed the introductions at the beginning of an important and lengthy meeting because I was due to speak in the middle of it. So, as arranged, I showed up halfway through. My job was to explain the storyboards for a commercial we were proposing to shoot. One of the clients smiled encouragingly throughout my presentation and so I devoted my entire attention to her.

At the end, I felt certain I had made a good impression. I had. Unfortunately, the client on whom I had focused turned out to be a new recruit to our agency whom I hadn't yet met. I had steadfastly ignored the real clients throughout the entire meeting.

There are two lessons to be learned. Look at everyone, ignore no one. And make sure you know who is in the room.

Involuntary Habits

When our nerves are active, we tend to become more physically active. We twitch, grimace, tug at our sleeves, brush invisible dust from the arms of our jacket, pace, run our hands through our hair, and any number of other involuntary mannerisms.

The best way to detect your particular display of nerves is to videotape yourself making a presentation and then study it. You may dread the prospect but I can assure you of two things. First, you won't look anywhere near as bad as you imagine. And secondly, you will be surprised by the number of unconscious mannerisms you have.

Some of them are merely distracting and should be avoided—jangling coins in your pocket, clicking a pen in your hand, scratching, constantly clearing your throat, cleaning and recleaning your glasses. You need to bring these activities into consciousness and then relax and let them go.

Other habits can be more distracting and send the wrong message. Crossing your arms looks defensive, pointing with an index finger or with something in your hand can look aggressive, rapid blinking looks frightened or bewildered, rubbing eyes suggests suspicion and loss of energy, while rubbing the back of your neck displays frustration.

There are also mannerisms that can be engaging in a pleasant way. You might appear thoughtful or reflective when stroking your chin or tilting your head. Hand-to-face gestures can suggest openness and a spirit of cooperation.

Mannerisms can mean different things when used by different people. The trick is to know your mannerisms so that you can exert some measure of conscious control.

If you can't face the cold eye of the camera, then get a friend or colleague to watch your presentation and list them. I don't think this is as powerful as seeing them for yourself. But it will give you a valuable insight. Best to pick someone you like and trust!

Dress and Appearance

Business cultures tend to have dress codes and you need to observe them or flout them for good reason.

> I spent much of my corporate life in the creative departments of advertising agencies. This branded me as someone who didn't know how to dress properly. "Creative" people have license to buck the system when it comes to dress and appearance. In fact, they are encouraged to do so. I was frequently the most casually dressed person in any meeting regardless of how far up the ladder we were working. I think some senior clients even found it reassuring.

But if you don't enjoy such a dispensation, you need to follow a simple rule.

Dress as well as the better-dressed people in the room.

> There can be no doubt that we judge people on appearances. If there is a particular impression you want to create, then dress accordingly. If not, follow the rule and you'll be greeted with a neutral response. People won't judge you one way or the other. And that's fine. This means they'll judge you on the quality of your presentation, and that is entirely within your control.

Summary and Action Points

The outer circle of the Planning Model contains the final process we need to follow when we are preparing a presentation.

There are only two key areas to address:

1. Verbal communication

Use your voice to communicate your Pathos—your passion for the subject.

Use it to control the mood of the meeting by varying the speed, pitch, and volume.

Talk in pictures and use your words to stimulate the sensory imagination of your listeners. Use analogies, metaphors, stories, and examples.

Use humor to engage and relax the audience, as long as it is appropriate.

2. Non-verbal communication

Bring your body language into your conscious awareness so that you can control it and use it to underscore your message.

Develop a "Rest Position" and be mindful of your gestures, facial expressions, eye movement, involuntary habits, dress, and appearance.

And finally, learn to relax and reduce your anxiety.

This not only makes your presentation more convincing, it will kill the dread and enable you to enjoy making it.

5. Conclusion

In her book, *Powerspeak*, Dorothy Leeds cites six common failings she has observed when watching other people give speeches and presentations.

They are these:

1. An Unclear Purpose
2. Lack of Clear Organization and Leadership
3. Too Much Information
4. Not Enough Support for Ideas and Concepts
5. Monotonous Voice and Sloppy Speech
6. Not Meeting the Real Needs of Your Audience

If you use the Who, the What, and the How of the Planning Model while preparing your presentation, you'll avoid them all.

A careful study of the Who will ensure you understand "The Real Needs of Your Audience." You'll know their preferred communication style and you'll know your own. You will be on their wavelength and you won't suffer from failing No. 6.

The inner circle, the What, will force you to have a clearly stated purpose and select only the information you need to support it. That information will then be put into the structure of the Organizational Diamond to make it comprehensible, memorable, and persuasive. That takes care of failing Nos. 1, 2, 3, and 4.

By practicing the How, the outermost ring of the Planning Model, you'll avoid failing No. 5. Your voice will not be monotonous and your speech will not be sloppy. Far from it. You'll use language that excites the imagination and the senses, and that engages the Whole Brain of your listeners. Not only that, but your gestures and movements will send messages that support and reinforce everything you are saying.

If this sounds like a lot to learn and a lot to do, then remember it's just a process. Start in the middle and work outward.

And practice.

The three laws of Real Estate are Location, Location, Location.

The three laws of Persuasive Presentation are Rehearse, Rehearse, Rehearse.

If you have the right material and it's well organized, if you have prepared the right visual support and you have rehearsed thoroughly, you'll take your audience on a journey that you all enjoy.

You won't feel nervous. You'll feel excited.

Index

Bibliography

The Creative Brain, Ned Herrmann, Ned Herrman Group

The Whole Brain Business Book, Ned Herrmann, McGraw-Hill

Persuading Aristotle, Peter Thomson, Kogan Page Ltd.

Powerspeak, Dorothy Leeds, Career Press

How to Mind Map, Tony Buzan, HarperCollins

The Business Presenter's Pocket Book, John Townsend, Management Pocket Books

How to Create and Deliver a Dynamic Presentation, Doug Malouf, American Society for Training & Development

A Lazy Man's Guide to Public Speaking, Mary Le Clair and Peter Fortune, Hyperion Books

Acknowledgments

The author would like to acknowledge the work of John Boyle at 6 Degrees. This book is based on his workshop training and principles of persuasion. All the models in this book are John's work and the author gratefully thanks John for his help in putting the material together. Thanks are also due to Kieran Ots, Glen MacNab, and Simon Cave for their fantastic work on designing the CD-ROM that accompanies this book.